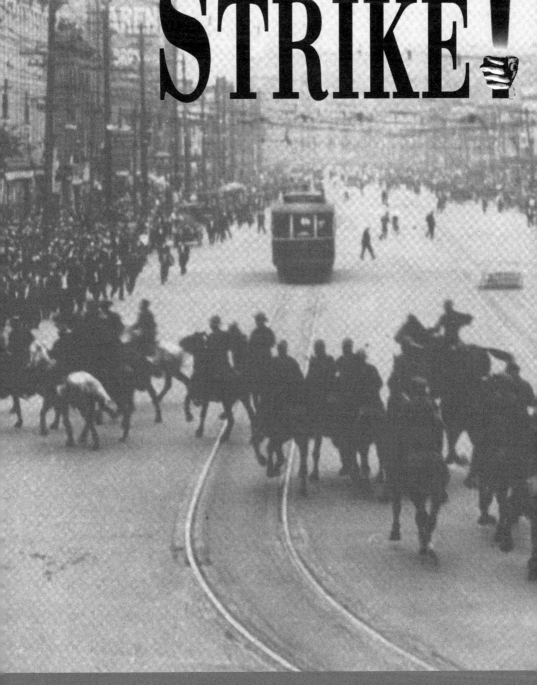

The Musical
STRIKE !

Script by
DANNY SCHUR & RICK CHAFE
Music and Lyrics by
DANNY SCHUR

Playwrights Canada Press
Toronto • Canada

Playwrights Canada Press
The Canadian Drama Publisher
215 Spadina Ave., Suite 230, Toronto, Ontario CANADA M5T 2C7
416.703.0013   fax 416.408.3402.
orders@playwrightscanada.com • www.playwrightscanada.com

This book would be twice its cover price were it not for the support of Canadian taxpayers
through the Government of Canada Book Publishing Industry Development Programme, Canada
Council for the Arts, Ontario Arts Council, and the Ontario Media Development Corporation.

Canada

Cover photos courtesy of the Manitoba Public Archives.
Cover design: Danny Schur/JLArt
Production Editor: MZK

Library and Archives Canada Cataloguing in Publication

Schur, Danny
    Strike! : the musical / Danny Schur.

A play.
Accompanied by a CD.
ISBN 978-0-88754-765-2

    1. General Strike, Winnipeg, Man., 1919--Drama. 2. Musicals--Librettos.
I. Chafe, Rick II. Title.

PS8637.C584S77 2007   C812'.6   C2007-905820-5

First edition: November 2007.
Printed and bound by Hignell Printing at Winnipeg, Manitoba, CANADA.

Table of Contents

Foreword

by Sharon & Nolan Reilly, Winnipeg, October 2007

In 1950 Jacob Penner, a participant in the Winnipeg General Strike, reminisced;

> The Winnipeg General Strike is immortal. It lives in the memory of those that are still with us and who took such an honourable part in the struggle for the rights of the producers of wealth. It lives in the memory of the sons and daughters of those that participated and to whom this story is being related by their parents during quiet family hours.

Danny Schur & Rick Chafe's play, *Strike! The Musical,* is the most recent in a long history of academic and popular interpretations of this dramatic episode in the history of modern Canada that have combined to ensure that Jacob Penner's words remained true. Since its outdoor preview at Winnipeg's Market Square in 2004, a short walk from the site where many of the key events of the 1919 Winnipeg General Strike occurred, *Strike!* has swept audiences off their feet.

On May 15th, 1919, 35,000 men, women and children walked off the job in a six-week long confrontation that brought life in Winnipeg to a standstill. Fought by working class families for the right to union recognition, shorter hours of work, and a living wage, the strike drew the attention of much of the industrialized world to Winnipeg.

Workers across the country and beyond took hope from the confrontation in Winnipeg, while government leaders and business elites viewed labour's unified demands with grave concern and wasted little time in responding to labour's challenge. Organized as the Citizens' Committee of 1000, Winnipeg's wealthiest manufacturers, lawyers, bankers, and politicians ignored the strikers' basic demands for improved wages and union recognition. Instead, they declared the strike a revolutionary conspiracy and branded the strikers as Bolsheviks and "alien scum." The Citizens' Committee had no evidence to support such charges, but used the accusations as a means to avoid conciliation.

The strike ended in bloodshed when government authorities used military force to establish their control over the city. Two workers died and many were injured in the events of "Bloody Saturday." Scores of workers lost their jobs and others were deported for supporting the strike. In the decades that followed, however, the struggle between the two factions continued, often taking place in the political arena. Although the events of 1919 left labour weakened in the workplace, it clearly strengthened the voice of working people at the ballot box. Labour candidates enjoyed electoral success over the next decade at every level of politics – school board, civic, provincial, and federal.

The intensity of the Winnipeg General Strike and the widespread revolt of labour across Canada in the immediate post-World War I era forced the established mainstream political parties to re-consider their attitudes towards the labour movement. The strike also had an important legacy on workers' attitudes towards how they wished to organize themselves. When the next big wave of union organizing that marked the origins of the modern labour movement began in the 1930s, workers chose industrial unions over craft coalitions.

Since the publication in 1920 of the strike leaders' treatise, "Address to the Jury," labour activists, historians, archivists, novelists, playwrights, musicians, documentary filmmakers, artists, museum curators, heritage proponents and others have sought to explore and interpret the events of 1919. In a multitude of ways, they have helped to ensure that Jacob Penner's prediction remained true.

Strike! has made a significant contribution to this undertaking, reawakening and generating new, widespread public interest in the Winnipeg General Strike. The production has caught the imagination of audiences not only because, as the first musical based upon the events of 1919, *Strike!* is highly entertaining but, also, because at its core is the historical nugget of Mike Sokolowski.

Through *Strike!* Schur and Chafe have retrieved this virtually unknown man, who died on the streets of Winnipeg on "Bloody Saturday," from the silence of history. Schur and Chafe have resurrected not only the death, but also the life of Mike Sokolowski, creating a compelling tragic hero and a complete cast of fictional characters based upon the possibilities presented by the diverse, immigrant neighbourhoods that existed in working class Winnipeg in 1919.

While the story that unfolds in *Strike!* with its young love and the struggle against both class oppression and social disapproval in the face of traditional ethnic divisions, is a work of fiction, it is one that raises important questions about the real Mike Sokolowski and the society in which he lived. More importantly, as demonstrated by the central role this musical plays in CBC's new, forward-looking documentary, "Bloody Saturday," *Strike!* gives audiences pause to think, perhaps in a new way, about basic human rights, participatory democracy, and the issues that continue to oppress working class and immigrant communities today.

● ● ●

Sharon Reilly is the curator of Social History at The Manitoba Museum.
Nolan Reilly is the chair of the Department of History at the University of Winnipeg.

Message from the Playwrights

by Danny Schur & Rick Chafe, Winnipeg, September 2007

Margaret Mead said that we can never underestimate the ability of a small group of committed citizens to change the world. *Strike!* is the story of the nation-changing 1919 Winnipeg General Strike, but also a fitting metaphor for our modern world of conflict. Tolerance and compromise are as necessary today as they were in 1919.

We would like to acknowledge the invaluable contributions of the following organizations and individuals: the Manitoba Association of Playwrights, University of Winnipeg Theatre Department, Mayworks Winnipeg, Platinum-Gold Studios Winnipeg, the Shevchenko Foundation, the Ukrainian Labour Temple Foundation, the Canada Council for the Arts, the Winnipeg Arts Council, the Manitoba Arts Council, Community Economic Development Corporation (Province of Manitoba), Arts Branch – Department of Culture (Province of Manitoba), The Winnipeg Foundation, the Canadian Broadcasting Corporation, Manitoba Film & Sound, Canadian Union of Public Employees, Ann Hodges, Tom Mokry, Rory Runnells, Brian Drader and, as always, Juliane Schaible & Martine Friesen.

Strike! premiered on May 26th, 2005 at Theatre in the Park in Winnipeg, Manitoba, produced by Danny Schur, with a cast of 21 and a chorus of 50, with the following company:

MIKE SOKOLOWSKI . . . . Jay Brazeau
STEFAN DUDAR . . . . Marc Devigne
REBECCA ALMAZOFF . . . . Catherine Wreford
MOISHE ALMAZOFF . . . . David Friedman
SENATOR GIDEON ROBERTSON . . . . Christopher Ryan
O'REILLY . . . . Carson Nattrass
CAPTAIN McDOUGALL . . . . Jon Ted Wynne
SUSAN ASHDOWN . . . . Melanie Whyte
JAMES ASHDOWN . . . . Stan Lesk
EMMA . . . . Sharon Bajer
UNION REP. . . . . Jeremy Koz
SUFFRAGETTE . . . . Dana Horrox
CARMICHAEL . . . . Kevin Aichele
MRS. OLYNYK . . . . Brenda Gorlick
MEETING LEADER / WALLACE . . . . Matt Kippen
BRONFMAN / McCREADY . . . . Taras Luchak
IMMIGRANT WOMAN . . . . Stacey Nattrass
VETERAN / SPECIAL . . . . Jeffrey Kohut
VETERAN / SPECIAL . . . . Tyson Wiebe
TELEPHONE OPERATOR . . . . Ilena Zaramba
TELEPHONE OPERATOR . . . . Cherise Kotelniski

Director . . . . Ann Hodges
Assistant to the Director & Choreographer . . . . . Tom Mokry
Musical Director & Orchestra Conductor . . . . Tusia Kozub
Additional Choreography . . . . Brenda Gorlick
Set Designer . . . . David Hewlett
Costume Designer . . . . Jan Malabar
Lighting Designer . . . . Scott Henderson
Stage Manager . . . . Paul Skirzyk
Assistant Stage Managers . . . . Amanda Smart
& Karla Trujillo Villon

Strike! was developed through a series of workshops sponsored by the Manitoba Association of Playwrights and the University of Winnipeg Theatre Department.

With doubling and line re-assignment, *Strike!* may be performed with as few as ten actors. *Strike!* opened in a modified version at Persephone Theatre in Saskatoon, Saskatchewan in September, 2006 with the following company:

MIKE SOKOLOWSKI .... Jeff Page

STEFAN DUDAR .... Marc Devigne

REBECCA ALMAZOFF .... Leora Joy Godden

MOISHE ALMAZOFF /
  RAILSHOP WORKER .... Mark Oddan

SENATOR GIDEON ROBERTSON /
  RAILWORKER .... Bruce McKay

O'REILLY / RAILSHOP REPRESENTATIVE /
  McCREADY .... Timothy Gledhill

CAPTAIN McDOUGALL .... Tim Hildebrand

SUSAN ASHDOWN / MRS. BRONFMAN /
  TELEPHONE OPERATOR .... Carol Wylie

CARMICHAEL/ JAMES ASHDOWN /
  WALLACE .... Jeff Pufahl

EMMA / MRS. OLYNYK / TELEPHONE
  OPERATORS' REPRESENTATIVE .... Deborah Buck

Director .... Ann Hodges
Choreographer .... Brenda Gorlick
Musical Director .... Deborah Buck
Set Designer .... Hans Becker
Costume Designer .... Theresa Germain
Lighting Designer .... Mark von Eschen
Stage Manager .... Laura Kennedy

Setting

Winnipeg, Manitoba, Canada
May – June 1919.

Pronunciation Key

Where indicated, vowels are round. "A" (transliterated "ah") is pronounced like the "a" in "car" and "o" (transliterated "oh") is like the "o" in "foreigner."

Main Characters

MIKE SOKOLOWSKI: (Soh-koh-LOW-skee) 45, Ukrainian Catholic immigrant; a railway worker.

STEFAN DUDAR: (Steh-FAHN Doo-DAR) 19, Ukrainian Catholic immigrant; Mike's godson.

REBECCA ALMAZOFF: (Ahl-MAH-zoff) 19, Jewish suffragette; Mike and Stefan's neighbour.

MOISHE ALMAZOFF: (MOY- sheh) 29, student and moderate Jewish community leader; Rebecca's brother.

SENATOR GIDEON ROBERTSON: 45, Federal Minister of Labour; sent on behalf of the Government of Canada to negotiate with the strikers.

JAMES ASHDOWN: 55, self-made Cockney millionaire and former mayor of Winnipeg; long-time family friend of Robertson.

SUSAN ASHDOWN: 50, supporter of worthy causes and pillar of the Methodist Church; wife of James Ashdown.

CAPTAIN McDOUGALL: 35, Scottish veteran now returned to job as police captain.

O'REILLY: 28, unemployed Irish veteran; fought alongside Captain McDougall.

EMMA, 25, the Ashdowns' Irish maid.

Additional Characters

CARMICHAEL
MEETING LEADER
MR. BRONFMAN
MRS. OLYNYK (Oh-LIN-ick)
A RAILWORKER
UNION REPRESENTATIVE
SUFFRAGETTE
FEMALE TELEPHONE OPERATORS
FEMALE TELEPHONE OPERATORS' REPRESENTATIVE
RAILSHOP WORKERS

RAILSHOP WORKERS' REPRESENTATIVE
IMMIGRANT WOMAN
WALLACE – a union member
McCREADY – a union member
STRIKERS
Newly-drafted temporary police (SPECIALS)
SOLDIERS
PEDDLER
SHOPKEEPER
POLICE OFFICERS

Music for the show is available for three- to ten-person orchestra, as well as on a vocal-removed accompaniment CD.

The script includes CD start cues to facilitate listening to the accompanying music while reading the script.

ACT ONE   Scene One

Portage Avenue, Winnipeg, Manitoba, Canada, late afternoon, May 1919.

There is not an undeveloped inch on Portage Avenue. Three-storey brick buildings, ornate banks with Corinthian columns and large arched windows, and small skyscrapers compete for space. Hydro and telegraph wires sag and snake above streetcar rails and Victorian streetlights. Poorly dressed immigrants and wealthy middle to upper class jostle for space on an avenue that bursts forth with optimism and enthusiasm.

Music begins. [Play CD Track #1 – "Winnipeg's Giddy."]

CHORUS   (*singing*) Winnipeg's giddy
It's 1919
There ain't been a city
With Winnipeg's gleam
Seams are a-burstin'
There's growth everywhere
The Prairies are thirstin' for
Winnipeg's wares
Flags are unfurled
Bring on the world
Winnipeg's giddy in 1919

MIKE SOKOLOWSKI and STEFAN DUDAR step off a streetcar, dressed in soft cloth caps. They don't get here often, and gawk at the crowd and the sights of Portage Avenue. MOISHE and REBECCA ALMAZOFF emerge through the crowd.

STEFAN   (*calling*) Miss Almazoff!

REBECCA looks back, unsure she's really heard her name called, but doesn't see STEFAN through the bodies.

MIKE   Hey, hey. I thought we got such an important meeting.

STEFAN   She's going too. We can walk together.

MIKE   You'll see her enough when you get there.

STEFAN   Why can't we keep her company?

MIKE   Why do you need company? You got me.

>   *MIKE pushes STEFAN along while REBECCA's brother, MOISHE, motions her to hurry.*

CHORUS

(singing) Winnipeg's giddy
It's 1919
There ain't been a city
With Winnipeg's gleam
The Great War is over
Our soldiers are home
More glorious victors
No one has known

>   *A unit of SOLDIERS marches by, including O'REILLY carrying a Union Jack. Two steps behind, one of the unit holds a large sign that reads "Deport the Enemy Alien." They salute the police officer, Captain McDOUGALL.*

Flags are unfurled
Bring on the world
Winnipeg's giddy in 1919

SOLDIERS & McDOUGALL

We stuck out our necks
Like some miserable drecks
And we fought tooth and nail
'Til the Krauts hid their tail
Then we up and come home
And our jobs have all flown to those
Damn immigrants
Where is the sense?
You tell me!

>   *The soldiers march again. CARMICHAEL gives STEFAN a shove.*

CARMICHAEL   Hey, ya dumb Uke. You're on the wrong side of the street.

MIKE   We're on the wrong side of the ocean.

CARMICHAEL   Just stay the hell out of the way.

MIKE   What's wrong? Your friend stopped counting steps? You got mixed up?

CARMICHAEL   You looking for a fight, Bohunk?

MIKE   Would I disrespect a fine soldier? Strong like bull. Smart like brick.

CARMICHAEL   Why I oughta…

O'REILLY pulls CARMICHAEL back into line. The unit marches on.

IMMIGRANTS, REBECCA, MOISHE, MIKE, STEFAN *(singing)*

> We left what was home
> For a promise of gold
> Now we slave night and day
> In the jobs that don't pay
> And our fam'lies we lose
> To that dread Spanish Flu from those
> Damn veterans
> Where is the sense?
> You tell me!

CHORUS

> Winnipeg's giddy
> It's 1919
> There ain't been a city
> With Winnipeg's gleam
> Seams are a-burstin'
> There's growth everywhere
> The Prairies are thirstin' for
> Winnipeg's wares
> Flags are unfurled
> Bring on the world
> Winnipeg's giddy in 1919
>
> Flags are unfurled
> Bring on the world
> Winnipeg's giddy in 1919

MIKE and STEFAN exit in the direction REBECCA and MOISHE have already taken. The street empties, with a number of immigrants becoming the crowd of The Meeting. Music ends.

ACT ONE   Scene Two

A meeting hall, immediately after.

Jewish and Ukrainian immigrants, including MOISHE and REBECCA ALMAZOFF, MR. BRONFMAN, MRS. OLYNYK and the MEETING LEADER, make a boisterous entrance. STEFAN DUDAR drags the unwilling MIKE SOKOLOWSKI by his sleeve. Outside the hall, a nervous Captain McDOUGALL keeps an eye on the goings-on.

STEFAN   Come on. You got this far. Come inside.

MIKE   Dis many Jews in one room. It makes me nervous.

STEFAN   Godfather. *(pointing at MIKE)* It's certain Ukrainians dat make me nervous.

> *STEFAN sees REBECCA and makes a beeline for her.*

Good evening, Miss Almazoff.

REBECCA   Good evening, Mister Dudar.

STEFAN   I think I saw you and your brother earlier today. In front of Moscovitzes.

REBECCA   Well that can't be, Mister Dudar. We were nowhere near there.

STEFAN   But… I'm sure it was you.

REBECCA   Couldn't be. If you had seen me, you would have said hello.

> *She casts him a cheeky smile and sits with MOISHE, leaving STEFAN embarrassed and unsure whether to follow.*

MEETING LEADER   Let's come to order, ladies and gentlemen…

> *MIKE pulls STEFAN to a seat across the room.*

Neighbours. We are on the verge of an historic occasion—

BRONFMAN   First we talk about the Ukrainian Bishop. The Bishop who preaches hate for Jews right from the pulpit.

MEETING LEADER   Please – I am saying we are about to make—

MIKE   Excuse me, please. All da Bishop said, *(crossing himself)* God bless him, was dat even though there is Pro-hi-bee-shen, the whiskey still flows from the barrels of the Jews.

STEFAN   *(to MIKE)* Quiet.

BRONFMAN   This from the Ukrainian, Sokolowski, who has seen the bottom of many whiskey bottles.

MEETING LEADER   Gentlemen—

MIKE   Sold to me by my Jewish neighbour, Mr. Bronfman.

MEETING LEADER   Comrades. That will be enough—

BRONFMAN   I work, I peddle from dawn 'til dusk while this fat Ukrainian sleeps.

MIKE   I admit it. I am twice the man you are Bronfman. Therefore I need twice the sleep.

MEETING LEADER   Thank you, Mister Sokolowski—

MIKE   But it's hard to sleep when the rental inspector—a Jew—specializes in throwing Ukrainians on the street.

STEFAN   *(to MIKE)* Would you shut up!

BRONFMAN   And the fact that the rent was not paid had nothing to do with it!

MEETING LEADER   Comrades, enough! Please put your differences behind you for one night.

BRONFMAN   How can we work with you people? We make agreements, you break them! We talk politely, you insult us!

MEETING LEADER   That is not the business of our meeting!

MIKE   It is called democracy!

STEFAN   *(to MIKE)* Stop it!

> *MIKE gestures innocence.*

MRS. OLYNYK   Gentlemen, enough! You work ten hours a day for next to nothing. I work six days a week and cannot feed my family. Every other street is ready to fight for better conditions. Now can we please elect our representative and get out of here?

MEETING LEADER   Thank you, Mrs. Olynyk. We have our nominees before us—

MIKE   No. Why are we talking about a strike?

MEETING LEADER   We have been over this—

MIKE   Shut down the whole city! Are you mad? The one chance I have here is a job and you want to throw it away for me. For what? To go back to prison camp? Understand this. They hate us. This great General Strike – you have not one hope of succeeding with.

MOISHE   *(standing)* My neighbour, Mister Sokolowski, is a passionate and eloquent speaker. And what's more, he is right. There is much against us. The factory owners. Our own government. There are so many who would stop us. Which means our interests are one.

> *Music begins. [Play CD Track #2 – "The Immigrants' Song."]*

We are not to fight. We are in the same boat. The same very leaky boat.

l to r: Jay Brazeau, Marc Devigne
Photo by Andrew Sikorsky

(singing)
Synagogue 'gainst
Church of God
Ukrainian versus Jew
But don't believe
Society
Can tell between the two

An immigrant is all they see
An alien, the enemy
An immigrant yes I may be but
Damn them all they
Can't take all my
Dignity

MRS. OLYNYK   Moishe Almazoff is right. During the Influenza, he and his sister, Rebecca, helped everyone the same. Even after they lost their father... did you once hear them ask "Ukrainian or Jew?"

(singing) Our street has seen
Too many weep
We've filled so many graves

Ukrainian, Jew
There are but few
Who haven't known some pain

MRS. OLYNYK & CHORUS
An immigrant is all they see
An alien, the enemy
Yes immigrants we all may be but
Seize the hour and
Show them our
Unity

Underscore music continues.

Outside the hall, a group of soldiers approaches, rifles in hand, Corporal O'REILLY and Private CARMICHAEL among them.

O'REILLY   For the love a God, Davey. The war's over.

CARMICHAEL   It's a long way from over, O'Reilly. Not when there's still the cleaning up to do.

O'REILLY   We didn't go over there just to come home and start again.

CARMICHAEL   Out of the way O'Reilly, or you're one of them.

The soldiers push past O'REILLY, who is left outside with Captain McDOUGALL.

O'REILLY   Captain McDougall. They're takin' the law into their own hands—

McDOUGALL   Looks fine from here, O'Reilly.

O'REILLY heads indoors while McDOUGALL stays outside.

CARMICHAEL   Well look at this. The stinkin' foreigners are spoutin' revolution.

MEETING LEADER   This is a democratic assembly—

CARMICHAEL   What the hell do you people know about democracy? This is Bolshevism.

MIKE   I am not a Bolshevik!

MRS. OLYNYK   You soldiers are decommissioned. Who is your commander?

CARMICHAEL   Hey, there's no leaders in a workers' revolution, right? A proletariat dictatorship—

STEFAN   What do you know about it?

MIKE   *(to STEFAN)* Shut up!

CARMICHAEL   *(turning on STEFAN)* Boys gave their blood and bones over there. And for what?

O'REILLY   All right. You've made your point, Davey—

CARMICHAEL   So you stinkin' foreigners can steal our jobs and piss on our graves with your filthy Red urine?

> *MIKE steps in, protecting STEFAN.*

MIKE   We are not Bolsheviks, I tell you.

CARMICHAEL   Then sing "God Save the King." Or so help me, I will bash your head in.

> *MIKE stands silent.*

Sing it, Bohunk!

> *CARMICHAEL rifle-butts MIKE in the stomach and MIKE falls on the ground. STEFAN moves to rush the soldier, his neighbours hold him back.*

MIKE   *(singing, barely audible)*
         God save our gracious King
         Long live our noble King
         God save the King!

> *MIKE stops, out of breath.*

STEFAN   Leave him alone!

> *CARMICHAEL poises his rifle butt above MIKE's head.*

CARMICHAEL   Sing!

MIKE   *(singing)*
         Send him victorious
         Happy and glorious
         Long to reign over us
         God save the King!

> *The soldiers laugh and applaud, except O'REILLY.*

CARMICHAEL   This strike of yours is off to a flying start! Come on, lads, the night's just begun!

> *The soldiers exit, kicking over furniture. STEFAN helps MIKE.*

MIKE   There. You see? Welcome to Kah-NAH-dah.

MIKE and STEFAN pass McDOUGALL and O'REILLY outside.

McDOUGALL   Take 'im on 'ome and there won't be any charges. Ya hear?

STEFAN   It's them that should be charged!

MIKE and STEFAN exit.

O'REILLY   *(to McDOUGALL)* They'll be destroying every immigrant house and shop they see.

McDOUGALL   You'd do better supportin' your own, O'Reilly.

O'REILLY   This is a shame on every last veteran.

McDOUGALL   I canna count the times men like them saved our skins over there – mine and yours, they did. They deserve our undying respect. And we'll be givin' it to 'em.

McDOUGALL and O'REILLY exit. The sound of rioting is heard in the distance.

ACT ONE   Scene Three

In the streets of North End Winnipeg, immediately after.

STEFAN holds MIKE as they stumble home. There are still soldiers rioting in the distance.

MIKE   *(singing drunkenly)* God save our noble king,
God save that hym-NOH-vay king. *[Ukrainian, roughly for: Shit-covered.]*

STEFAN   You are an idiot.

MIKE   Lucky for you my stomach is bigger than your mouth.

STEFAN   They beat us up in prison camps, they beat us up on the streets – enough!

They arrive at their tenement house, a side-by-side with a porch they share with the Almazoffs, divided by a railing.

MIKE   Now you know how the world works. You can thank me later. Come write my letter.

MIKE goes in the front door.

STEFAN   First you apologize to the Almazoffs.

Laughing, MIKE comes out with a paper, pencil, and envelope.

MIKE   Okay, if that's what you want.

STEFAN   That's what I want.

MIKE   *(calling)* I'm sorry, Jew neighbours! My godson means well but he is an idiot!

STEFAN   This is what I mean—

MIKE   There are spies everywhere. If you keep making friends with Bolsheviki Jews, we will both be deported with them.

STEFAN   You always say do nothing. For once, I want to make a difference.

MIKE   You'll make a difference. You'll make everything worse. *(softening a bit)* I promised your parents I'd take care of you. No more meetings, yeah?

He hands pencil and paper to STEFAN.

Music begins. [Play CD Track #3 – "Dearest Anna."]

Now write.

STEFAN writes as MIKE sings.

> Dearest Anna
> How is dat Demyan?
> He was but so young
> Now somehow
> Writing his name

STEFAN   He should be learning to write in English – learning to write better than I do.

MIKE   Yeah yeah. Taras and Tekla. Fifth birthday next week. And he's chasing her around scaring her—

STEFAN   —with a dead gopher, yeah yeah.

MIKE   Little bugger. Like you.

They take up the writing again.

> Anna listen
> I'll get more shifts in
> My foreman's gift is

> He promised more
> Work in spring

STEFAN   It is spring.

MIKE   A few weeks left.

STEFAN   We're a long way back in line.

MIKE   Yeah, yeah.

> Sorry Anna
> It's not much money
> God knows I tried
> These are some
> Unlucky times

Music ends. MIKE takes money from his pocket, hands it to STEFAN to go with the letter.

Here.

STEFAN   *(taking it)* Five dollars? But you had at least—

MIKE   Just fifty more, we'll get there.

STEFAN   Christ, all your booze.

MIKE   *(moving to the door)* Some extra shifts. We'll have enough to bring all of them.

STEFAN   Yeah, Mike. Don't stay up too late, eh?

MIKE   Me? I don't sleep. A machine doesn't need sleep.

MIKE goes inside. STEFAN stays on the porch with MIKE's letter. REBECCA peeks her head out of her door.

REBECCA   Is your godfather all right?

STEFAN   I'm sure he's curing himself with a bit of whiskey. Sorry about your meeting.

REBECCA   There'll be another one.

STEFAN   I thought you liked meetings.

REBECCA   I would if I ever got to say anything.

STEFAN   I think I'd rather listen to you than your brother.

She smiles, he's an awkward flirt, but cute.

REBECCA   Moishe loves talking about rights for women. Just not any of the women he knows.

MOISHE strides up the street heading for the apartment door.

MOISHE   It's turned into a riot. They destroyed half the North End.

STEFAN   God damn them!

MOISHE   I'll be working all night.

STEFAN   Mr. Almazoff.... The English papers never report these things. Why aren't you writing about it for them?

MOISHE   Ask yourself, if they're interested in what I have to say.

STEFAN   You're a great writer—

MOISHE   Oh, you read Yiddish?

STEFAN   No, I just—

REBECCA   The English papers think he's a radical.

STEFAN   But... you are.

MOISHE   No, not at all.

STEFAN   You're the most radical person I know.

Music begins. [Play CD Track #4 – "Nothing Radical."]

MOISHE   No offence, Mr. Dudar, but your world is not that big.

STEFAN   You stand for revolution.

MOISHE   What.... No!

STEFAN   I thought you wanted to overthrow the—

MOISHE   You've completely misunderstood me.

STEFAN   But everything you say—

MOISHE   No!

> I'm for
> Living wages and
> Change in stages and
> Fundamental improvements for
> All the working class
> *(pointing to REBECCA)* Every working lass
> *(pointing to STEFAN)* Every head in soft hat
> There is

>Nothing radical, no
>Nothing radical
>Nothing radical about that

STEFAN   That's not what they say.

MOISHE   What do they say?

STEFAN   *(to REBECCA)* What you told me.

REBECCA   What everyone says. That you're a dangerous Bolshevik.

MOISHE   If you are asking if I am for armed revolution, sir, I am not...

>I'm for the
>Right to fraternize

REBECCA   And to unionize

MOISHE   And incremental adjustments for

REBECCA   Fairer bargaining

MOISHE   Lesser arguing

REBECCA   Worker spirits intact

MOISHE   There is
>Nothing radical, no

REBECCA   Nothing radical

MOISHE   Nothing radical about that.
>I'm not for
>Bloodshed or angry mobs

REBECCA   Hate-spreading ideologues

MOISHE   Radical policies that

REBECCA   Frighten authorities

MOISHE   Class wars and bigotry

REBECCA   Racists and zealotry

MOISHE   These I'm simply not for

STEFAN   Of course not, but what do we do about it?

MOISHE   We keep fighting for—

>Shorter working days
>Paid-for holidays
>Equal work: equal pay and for—

STEFAN	Safer working places
REBECCA	Fewer hungry faces

MOISHE   Decent jobs for the taking
There is
Nothing radical, no
Nothing radical
Nothing radical about that

STEFAN   Then whatever it is you are, I'm one of those too.

MOISHE, STEFAN & REBECCA
There is
Nothing radical, no
Nothing radical
Nothing radical about that

Music ends.

MIKE   *(offstage)* Almazoff. Shah-dup and go to bed.

MOISHE   Dah-vye, Rebecca. Good night, Mister Dudar. *[Dah-vye, Rebecca – Russian for: Come, Rebecca.]*

STEFAN   What about a letter to the editor?

MOISHE   A what?

STEFAN   I could write about the soldiers rioting, if you would help me?

MOISHE   Mr. Dudar. I'm not ready to be deported, are you?

STEFAN   I said I would write it. Who said anything about signing it?

REBECCA   I will help him.

MOISHE   No, you won't.

REBECCA   He's Ukrainian after all. All heart, less… education.

STEFAN   *Oiy!* Your sister is a Jew and a woman. Two times the mouth.

REBECCA   Well then we should make a very good team.

MOISHE   Rebecca, stop it.

REBECCA   *(defiantly)* Yes? What?

MOISHE   You know what I mean.

REBECCA   If you want to say something, say it to his face.

MOISHE   *(beat)* Don't play at this.

MOISHE enters the house.

STEFAN   I didn't mean to start the Great War all over again.

REBECCA   Moishe always thinks he's right.

STEFAN   Well. He's not right about this letter.

REBECCA   Of course he is. It's completely dangerous. Start it, "Dear Mr. Editor."

Uncertainly, STEFAN writes.

STEFAN   Uh… "Owing to our unfair classification as anti-allies…"

REBECCA   Unjust.

STEFAN   Unjust?

REBECCA   Unjust.

STEFAN   *(making the change)* Okay if you want unjust, it can be unjust.

As he begins making the change, she moves to STEFAN's porch. He surrenders the pencil to her.

REBECCA   *(writing)* "Dear Editor…. New immigrants to this country continue to be unjustly classified as enemy aliens…

l to r: Catherine Wreford, Marc Devigne
Photo by Andrew Sikorsky

> *Behind them, MIKE comes to the screen door. He watches and listens.*

…Intolerance and hatred of everything that is foreign has been planted in the public mind…"

STEFAN   Wow…

REBECCA   "…by irresponsible utterances in the press…"

MIKE   If your father were alive, he would be very disappointed, Miss Almazoff.

> *STEFAN and REBECCA separate, MIKE steps out onto the porch.*

He'd probably grab my dear godson by the neck *(grabs him by the scuff of the neck)* and call him a Shay-getz *[male Gentile]* or Shkutz *[male scum]*. And then he'd say, "Get away from my daughter and don't come near her again."

> *He flings STEFAN towards their door.*

(to both of them) Get inside.

> *REBECCA exits to her apartment.*

STEFAN   Stop treating me like a child. Now.

MIKE   Then grow up.

> *STEFAN goes in. MIKE stays a moment on the porch. Captain McDOUGALL passes by, patrolling the immigrant section. MIKE averts his eyes, then exits down the street.*

> *STEFAN, wearing a jacket and carrying a cap, steps quietly onto his porch, leans across the railing to knock on the Almazoff's window. REBECCA steps out onto the porch.*

STEFAN   *(holding up a piece of paper)* I'll finish it and get it to the newspaper office.

REBECCA   *(holding up the original)* Mine's probably better.

> *She hands him the letter.*

STEFAN   *(putting on his cap)* Wish me luck.

REBECCA   *(stepping out, already in her coat)* Good luck.

STEFAN   You can't come—

REBECCA   Try and stop me.

> *He smiles. They exit together.*

Act One   Scene Four

Portage Avenue, a few days later.

O'REILLY enters, his head buried in the Help Wanted section of a newspaper. Captain McDOUGALL enters from the other direction.

McDOUGALL   Didn't bein' a soldier teach ya to keep your head up, O'Reilly?

O'REILLY   Aye. But me heart is set sure on gettin' a job. A good one like yours.

McDOUGALL   Fat chance a that. You're competin' wi' boatloads of Bohunks, Krauts and Kikes lappin' up the jobs like flies ta shit. That's the problem wi' dis country. There ain't proper treatment of decorated veterans such as us.

O'REILLY   Aye. I suppose you're right.

O'REILLY continues to scan the paper and McDOUGALL notices the letters page.

l to r: Carson Nattrass, Jon Ted Wynne
Photo by Andrew Sikorsky

McDOUGALL   For the love a God! Would ya look at this? "Immigrants Protest the Soldiers Riot."

O'REILLY   Where?

McDOUGALL   "While the police stood by watching?"

O'REILLY   What are ya talkin'—

McDOUGALL   A riot they call it? How about a provoked action? Some bloody immigrant writes a letter without even the guts to sign it. Men give their lives and that's not good enough. *(exiting)* And now this is our homecoming.

> *As O'REILLY exits, MIKE and STEFAN enter in work clothes, carrying lunchboxes, with another RAILWORKER, who reads from a newspaper.*

RAILWORKER   You say there's no democracy in this country, Sokolowski? *(reading)* "New immigrants to this country continue to be unjustly classified as enemy aliens. Intolerance and hatred of everything that is foreign has been planted in the public mind by irresponsible utterances in the press..."

MIKE   What the hell is that?

RAILWORKER   "...resulting now in attacks from our own Canadian soldiers on our own land while police stood by watching..."

MIKE   Who wrote that?

RAILWORKER   "A concerned immigrant." Someone had the guts to tell the truth right in the paper.

> *MIKE looks up and sees STEFAN, staring back stupidly.*

MIKE   Teh whoo-yoo [*the "wh" sound pronounced like the "ch" in "Loch Lomand." Ukrainian, roughly for: You stupid prick.*]

RAILWORKER   Oh God.

MIKE   The hell now?

RAILWORKER   The Russian Army has crossed the border into Ukraine.

MIKE   Where?

> *STEFAN grabs the paper.*

STEFAN   That's all it says. One paragraph.

MIKE   Oh God.... Oh Jesus...

RAILWORKER   I... I have an extra shift tonight. You can have it.

MIKE   Yes...

STEFAN   We both will. I'll get a shift from someone.

RAILWORKER   I'll ask around.

> *RAILWORKER exits.*

STEFAN   Mike...

> *He puts a hand on MIKE's shoulder. MIKE shrugs it off. They exit.*

ACT ONE   Scene Five

> *Ashdown mansion living room.*
>
> *Music begins. [Play CD Track #5 – "Me Ma'am is Mum."]*
>
> *EMMA, the Ashdown's maid enters, talking on the telephone.*

EMMA   Molly. It's Emma. Can ya talk? The coast is clear.

> Well, me ma'am is mum
> And it strikes me kinda dumb
> 'Cause it just ain't her, not a bit
> When she swallows shit
> And she takes it in the tit
> From dat arse husband of 'ers

I don't care if he was his bloody worship the mayor!

> When me ma'am is mum
> I can't stand her playing dumb
> While his mouth spouts out loads of crap
> But I shuts me trap
> Or I'd get a bloody slap
> "Shut yer mouth Emma," says I
> Well I try
> Canna hide
> All dis here dat's bottled up inside

> Well I ain't the Queen of Scots
> But I been around the block
> And I know when such a ting is wrong

Then this morning paper comes, and ain't it stirred the nest! This wee letter's got her in a state.

> And still me ma'am is mum
> And she's turned a sour plum
> 'Cause her Mister says, "Leave it lie"
> Well, "Jesus Christ" says I
> "Canna woman speak her mind?
> Where's the muzzle strung on her?"

And didn't he turn on me set to box me brains?

The doorbell rings; EMMA doesn't notice.

> Woah, me ma'am is mum
> There's an anger there and some
> Like a beet she's red, then she blows
> "Have a heart," she crows
> And she tells him where to go
> And defends a one like me
> You shoulda seen
> I nearly peed
> Who'd tink a letter coulda caused a scene!?!

> Well she ain't the Queen of Scots
> But give 'er credit, give 'er lots
> 'Cause she knows a ting you can't ignore

JAMES and SUSAN ASHDOWN enter, arguing. EMMA hides the phone behind her back and the ASHDOWNS are in such a state they pass right by her.

SUSAN   I am simply asking you to see my point! The police should have intervened—

Doorbell rings.

JAMES   You've made your point at least fifty times and I've agreed!

SUSAN   You haven't agreed! You haven't even listened, you ass!

They exit.

EMMA   Whoa, Molly, the pump's been primed!

> Might me ma'am be mum no more?

Music ends. Doorbell rings. The ASHDOWNS re-enter. EMMA is stuck with the phone behind her back.

SUSAN   You are the most pigheaded obstinate brute of a—

Senator ROBERTSON steps into the room, unnoticed by any of them.

JAMES Between you and the screeching Bolshie maid, why don't we just open up strike headquarters right here in the living room?

ROBERTSON Forgive my arriving unannounced.

EMMA The Minister of Labour to see you, sir.

JAMES Senator Robertson!

SUSAN Gideon.

ROBERTSON I tried calling but your telephone has been engaged a full half hour.

JAMES Bit early in the day – were you hoping for breakfast?

SUSAN Tea, Emma.

EMMA Yes, ma'am.

ROBERTSON *(displaying the newspaper)* You haven't seen this?

EMMA stops to listen.

JAMES Susan's just been sharing her views on it.

SUSAN Tea, Emma.

EMMA Yes, ma'am.

EMMA reluctantly exits.

ROBERTSON The timing could not be worse. All this strike business in the air, and the bloody paper has the idiocy to print this?

Music begins. [Play CD Track #6 – "Plight of the Working Class."]

James, I want your help and your influence on this from this moment on.

JAMES You have it already, of course.

SUSAN It's just a letter, Gideon, it's hardly a declaration of war.

ROBERTSON That's exactly what it is, Susan, I couldn't have put it better.

EMMA re-appears with the tea, having hurried not to miss a thing.

> *(singing)* As a union man in the rail trades
> I've walked in labour's shoes
> But as a minister of Parliament
> I've tough measures to choose

> These radicals would seize the day
> And push us way too far
> The trouble can be rid of quick
> If we remove the cause
>
> The right of the ruling class
> Demands that the gov'rn-ment act
> To spare society the pain
> The right of the ruling class
> Is to put down the working class
> Before revolution wins the day

JAMES   Revolution's a bit strong, Gideon. You have to realize the veterans' rioting is a sore point.

SUSAN   Not to mention the police—

JAMES   Not to mention the police, refusing to lift a finger. It's a bit of a black eye for the city.

ROBERTSON   Completely agreed. The behaviour of these soldiers is deplorable, but who can blame them? The immigrants have turned this city into a powder keg and this strike would light the fuse.

JAMES   It comes down to jobs and decent wages. You have to meet them at the table, Gideon.

ROBERTSON   Negotiate over an illegal strike? I most certainly will not!

JAMES   *(singing)* Born to a family of lesser means
> I feel for the common man
> I walked five hundred miles to here
> Not a penny in my hand
> And all we've won through all these years
> We share with those in need
> But charities grow useless with
> So many mouths to feed
>
> The plight of the working class
> Demands that we all must act
> To spare society the pain

SUSAN & JAMES   The plight of the working class
> Must dwell in the distant past
> Before revolution wins the day

ROBERTSON   James. Our prime minister is sitting at a table in Paris this very moment.

JAMES   I'm aware of it.

ROBERTSON   Across from the British prime minister and the American president. Trying to clean up the mess the war has left us in. The last thing he needs is an outbreak of Bolshevism in his own backyard.

JAMES   All right. Point taken, of course.

ROBERTSON   *(singing)* Our families are the best of friends…

JAMES   And been so many years

ROBERTSON   Your influence is dear to me…

JAMES   And you're welcomed among peers

ROBERTSON   And if this thing's to simmer down
I could use your heft
Deporting Bol-shee immigrants…
Is the only option left
The right of the ruling class

JAMES   Demands that the gov'rn-ment act

JAMES & ROBERTSON
To spare society the pain

JAMES   The right of the ruling class

ROBERTSON   Is to put down the working class

JAMES & ROBERTSON
Before revolution wins the day

   Music ends.

ROBERTSON   And we'll start by making a swift and very public example of the writer of this letter.

JAMES   You have our support, Gideon.

EMMA   Ma'am—

SUSAN   Kitchen, Emma.

EMMA   Yes, ma'am.

   EMMA heads off, but stops before leaving the stage.

ROBERTSON   Well I appreciate it, James. Susan.

JAMES   Always, Gideon.

   ROBERTSON and JAMES exit.

EMMA   Ma'am? What's it mean, they'll make an example?

SUSAN   The letter writer will be sent packing.

EMMA   Deported? For writing a letter to the newspaper?

SUSAN   It's not an easy job to run a country, Emma. No easier than James had when he was running this city.

EMMA   But ma'am… you didn't say a word…

SUSAN   I've said quite a lot of words. Having them heard is the problem.

> *SUSAN exits and EMMA follows a moment later.*

ACT ONE   Scene Six

> *Government Telephones Building, immediately after.*
>
> *Music begins. [Play CD Track #7 – "Fifty Dollars."]*
>
> *A dreary interior with single-shaded bulbs hanging from long wires. Women wearing headphones are seated in rolling office chairs at a telephone switchboard, murmuring with callers and patching calls. REBECCA enters wearily, hangs her coat.*

REBECCA
Fifty dollars
Fifty dollars
Fifty dollars
In a half a year

> *She makes her way over to her spot at the switchboard, seats herself and begins the repetitive task of connecting and disconnecting the lines.*

Repetition
Promotes attrition
Of all the hopes and dreams that
I did see when
I was but a
Girl with thoughts that
Some day there could
Be a world in
Which it wouldn't
Matter just how
Much my worth in dollars made but

Now I see the fool I've played 'cause
All my work is paid is

Fifty dollars
Fifty dollars

OPERATOR # 1   She makes

REBECCA   Fifty dollars
In a half a year

ALL   Fifty dollars
Fifty dollars

She makes
Fifty dollars
In a half a year

Railway shop, at the same time.

A dusty railway repair shop. MIKE, STEFAN, and other proud but dirty RAILSHOP WORKERS bang away at oversized railcar parts with large ball-peen hammers. Their hammering forms a chain gang rhythm with the music. MIKE is exhausted and breaks from the monotony while the others continue.

MIKE   Immigration:
Cancellation
Of all the hopes and dreams that
I did see when
I was still a
Man with wife and
Children who would
Fill my world with
Love because it
Mattered not how
Much my love in dollars brought but
Now they run from Bohl-sheh-veks
'Cause all that I can make is

Eighty dollars
Eighty dollars

RAILSHOP WORKERS
He makes

MIKE   Eighty dollars
In a half a year

> *The rest of the male workers join MIKE in singing. The telephone OPERATORS join as well but continue to sing "Fifty dollars."*

ALL
Eighty [fifty] dollars
Eighty [fifty] dollars

We make
Eighty [fifty] dollars
In a half a year

A six-month contract's the best that we're offered
But cost of living has risen by eighty per cent:
Not one cent
Come the rent

> *A female TELEPHONE OPERATORS' REPRESENTATIVE enters into the switchboard room while, in the railway shop, a male RAILSHOP WORKERS' REPRESENTATIVE enters there.*

OPERATORS' REP   *(excited but worried)* Girls. I've got big news.

> *Chattering.*

RAILSHOP REP   It looks like things have come to a head, boys.

OPERATORS' REP   The bosses won't recognize collective bargaining or increase wages.

> *Mutterings from both shops.*

RAILSHOP REP   For the sake of labour everywhere, it's time we stepped up.

OPERATORS' REP   The Trades and Labour Council has asked for a vote on a General Strike.

RAILSHOP REP   I know things are real tough for some of you boys, but we all stand to win here.

MIKE   What business do we have talking strike?

OPERATORS' REP   Even the non-union shops are voting to support us.

MIKE   Let the unions slit their own throats! We don't have to cut ours as well!

RAILSHOP REP   Union and non-union, we can show them real solidarity. A whole city shut down if we go out together.

MIKE   I cannot be on strike!

OPERATORS' REP   Can we have a show of hands?

The OPERATORS look around the room.

MIKE   I have a wife and children in the Old Country—

RAILSHOP REP   What'll it be then boys?

> *Some of the OPERATORS, including REBECCA, are slow to put up their hands, as if doing so was dangerous. Eventually all have put up their hands and a wave of smiles and militancy sweeps their room. In the railway shop, all hands go up quickly, including MIKE's RAILWORKER friend.*

STEFAN   I'm sorry, Mike.

> *STEFAN lifts his hand.*

MIKE   Christ…

> *MIKE stares, then exits.*

ALL   (singing)
Sixty [Ninety] dollars now that would be something
Sixty [Ninety] dollars now that would just be the day
That would pay
A living wage
We just want
Sixty [ninety] dollars
Sixty [ninety] dollars

We need
Sixty [ninety] dollars
For the half a year
Just sixty [ninety] dollars
For the half a year

> *There are frightened but hopeful looks as everyone returns to work.*

> *Solo light on MIKE.*

MIKE   Dearest Anna
Just fifty dollars
Then our fam-ly
Runs from that
Bolshevik army

> *Lights fade out. Music ends.*

Act One   Scene Seven

> Portage Avenue.
>
> Music begins. [Play CD Track #8 – "A Better Man."]
>
> SUSAN ASHDOWN enters, holding a collection pot. Captain McDOUGALL enters, walking his beat.

SUSAN   (to McDOUGALL) Support the veterans' fund?

> McDOUGALL is digging in his pocket when a poor IMMIGRANT WOMAN enters.

IMMIGRANT WOMAN   Proh-shoo. Hroh-shee. [Ukrainian: Please. Money.]

> McDOUGALL drops his coins in the collection pot and turns to the woman.

McDOUGALL   I told ya the next time we'd hafta arrest ya.

IMMIGRANT WOMAN   No, no please.

> He rough-handles the IMMIGRANT WOMAN off.

McDOUGALL   (to SUSAN) I'm sorry you have to witness it, ma'am. Them beggar-women come back as soon as you can clear 'em out.

SUSAN   (singing) Charity is loathsome
When the cause is not one's own
Yet here I stand and smile and stew
'Til bitter to the bone
I see widows' children starving
From the war that's torn the land
But God forbid a woman speaks
She must heed the better man

A better man
I gave my hand
To a better man
I abandoned plans
My husband shines of decency
And so politely hinders me
My role is far beneath
The better man

SUSAN continues her petitions to walkers-by. REBECCA enters at the Almazoff porch.

REBECCA

Overnight a whole new world
With exciting goings-on
Life grows in complexity
Now a man has come along
I'm dying just to touch him
But forget such naïve plans
A Catholic is forbidden fruit
They tell me find a better man
A better man

SUSAN

Have I no voice?

REBECCA

"It's God's own plan"

SUSAN

So little choice

REBECCA

A better man

SUSAN

The times have changed

REBECCA

Or I'll be damned

SUSAN

Yet I've remained

REBECCA

Whispered words of mockery
Won't change my choice of man for me
They can't dictate who'll be
My better man

SUSAN and REBECCA remain. MIKE approaches the Police Station.

MIKE

I've tried to be a good man
I bear my crosses everyday
I always take the sacraments
And pray God spares my name
But I've run out of choices

Captain McDOUGALL steps out of the Police Station.

I'm forced to take this path
Lord you must forgive me now
You've lost a better man

Captain.... They say you're buying information.

McDOUGALL   What have you got?

MIKE   How much do you pay?

McDOUGALL   I think you better tell me what you're selling.

MIKE   I need fifty dollars.

McDOUGALL   Fifty? Turning in the Kaiser would get you ten.

MIKE   Fifty.

McDOUGALL   And what is worth fifty dollars?

MIKE   I know who wrote that letter.

McDOUGALL   We'll see. Wait here. (*He exits back into the police station.*)

> *MIKE, REBECCA and SUSAN sing but they are in three separate universes.*

MIKE	A better man
SUSAN	What's wrong with me?
MIKE	I'm hardly dat
REBECCA	Am I not free?
MIKE	I sell my soul
SUSAN & REBECCA	
	My deepest need
MIKE	To have them home
ALL	It's killing me
SUSAN & REBECCA	
	Freedom is the goal I seek
MIKE	I'll die without my family
	Dear God, could I still be
REBECCA	Who chooses for me
SUSAN	Could a woman be

Singing simultaneously:

MIKE	**REBECCA**	**SUSAN**
A better man?	My better man?	The better man?

> *Music ends.*

ACT ONE   Scene Eight

Sokolowski / Almazoff house, that evening.

REBECCA enters in her work clothes, carrying her coat. She doesn't go in yet – nice weather starts late in Winnipeg. She settles on the porch to enjoy it. A moment later, STEFAN arrives with his lunch box. He hesitates seeing REBECCA, uncertain how to say what he has to.

REBECCA   No late shift, Mr. Dudar?

STEFAN   No.

He sits beside her.

REBECCA   You won't have to work inside during this beautiful spring weather. They finished counting votes. Eleven o'clock tomorrow the whole city stops working.

STEFAN   Good. That's good.

REBECCA   *(pause, tries teasing to draw him out)* I told a friend of mine about a nice boy I met. She said, "Does he go to our synagogue?" I said, "He doesn't go to synagogue." She said, "You make sure he starts." I said, "I don't think so." "Why doesn't he go to shul," she said. I said, "Because he's Catholic." She said, "You didn't let him kiss you, did you?" I said, "When it comes to kissing, I'm not sure there's much danger."

STEFAN   I... talked to someone too.

REBECCA   Who?

STEFAN   My priest.

REBECCA   Why?

STEFAN   It's what Catholics do. We confess our sins.

REBECCA   What sin? The letter?

STEFAN   No—

REBECCA   You told?

STEFAN   No! I mean, yes, I did, but it's—

REBECCA   You told your priest?

STEFAN   You can trust a priest.

REBECCA   Why would you tell him about the letter?

STEFAN   I wasn't confessing the letter, it just came out.

REBECCA   But what were you—

STEFAN   I'm trying to tell you! Then yesterday at mass. When we were taking communion. Everyone's kneeling at the front of the church. The priest brings the Body of Christ in the bread and wine. But when he came to me, he said, "You, no." In front of Mike. In front of every Ukrainian I know. He said, "Communion isn't for Jews."

> *Pause.*

REBECCA   So it was me you confessed. I'm the sin.

STEFAN   A Catholic can't marry a Jew.

REBECCA   Who's marrying anyone?

STEFAN   I had to find out what you would have to do to convert.

REBECCA   *Oiy!* I'm not converting.

STEFAN   You have to.

REBECCA   I do not! I don't even believe in marriage.

STEFAN   Everyone believes in marriage.

REBECCA   It's stupid, it's old fashioned, this is the twentieth century—

STEFAN   What are *you* talking about?

REBECCA   What are you talking about? You haven't even tried to hold my hand yet!

> *STEFAN reaches for her hand.*

So we hold hands and then we kiss and then we do whatever the priest tells us? We convert the Jew and the problem is solved?

> *They don't notice two men approaching – union men WALLACE and McCREADY.*

STEFAN   HOS-poh-deh, *[Ukrainian, roughly for God in Heaven.]* what do you want from me?

McCREADY   Stefan Dudar?

STEFAN   *(turning, a little frightened)* You know my name. What do you want?

WALLACE   There are nasty rumours floating.

STEFAN   Rumours float well in this city.

WALLACE   But these concern you, Steven.

REBECCA   What is he rumoured to be doing?

McCREADY   Talk with you privately, Stefan?

STEFAN   Talk to us both.

McCREADY   We have a good idea you wrote that letter to the paper.

WALLACE   And what with the strike coming to pass, they're going to be looking to string up a foreigner, even if it's just for show.

STEFAN   And so why do you tell me this?

McCREADY   The long and short of it is; if a man such as you has the guts to stand up for what's right... even if you are a Catholic, for Chrissakes... well, then they're going to have to come through us to get to you.

WALLACE   We'll be watching your back for a while. You got our protection.

STEFAN   You'd help a Ukrainian?

WALLACE   You Ukes don't have much brains, it's true, but you're hard enough workers. I guess I won't mind too bad.

McCREADY   One of the boys will be watchin' out for you at all times. All right?

WALLACE   Don't you worry Steve. We're with you.

> *WALLACE and McCREADY tip their hats toward REBECCA and exit.*

REBECCA   My God.

STEFAN   Oiy BOH-zheh.... *[Ukrainian: Oh God.]*

REBECCA   Yes. You can trust a priest.

STEFAN   The priest wouldn't tell—

REBECCA   Who else knows?

STEFAN   No one—

REBECCA   Ida Stein told her mother, "Rebecca has a Catholic boyfriend." Her mother looked straight at me and said, "A Catholic and a Jew. People have been killed for less."

STEFAN   That's not going to happen—

REBECCA   I know what I'm talking about. I am from Ukraine too. Did you murder any Jews in the pogroms?

STEFAN   No! We left when I was fourteen!

REBECCA   I'm sorry. Your people and mine are not friends. And now you need a bodyguard. No one's going to celebrate our friendship, Stefan.

STEFAN   Just us.

REBECCA   Will we?

> *Music begins. [Play CD Track #9 – "Love in a Place Like This."]*

STEFAN   (*singing*) We're wrong for each other
You're right as can be
Same side of the tracks
But still worlds between
As far as I can see
No one wants us to be
But the world is full of no's

REBECCA   Constant reminders of
Something so doomed
Hurtful suggestions
And thought of as fools
Each voice that I hear
Warns me "Stay clear"
How can my heart find home?

STEFAN & REBECCA
How can there be love?
Love in a place like this?
Who wants to take the risk
On love in a place like this?
One possible fate
Surely awaits
Love in a place like this

STEFAN   We're not so different
There's much that we share
We yearn for the same things
We burn for what's fair
I know deep inside
Your heart is like mine
For this I feel no shame

REBECCA Noble intentions
Of fools unaware
Still leave me with scars
And a heart that's just scared
They'd make it a shame
Just to mention our name
Can you handle so much pain?

STEFAN & REBECCA
How can there be love?
Love in a place like this?
Who wants to take the risk
On love in a place like this?
One possible fate
Surely awaits
Love in a place like this

Maybe there's someone who's brave enough to try
To break the mould and make a world
Where love is truly blind

Maybe there'll be love?
Love in a place like this?
Who wants to take the risk
On love in a place like this?
One possible fate
Surely awaits
Love in a place like this

One possible fate
Surely awaits
Love in a place like this

STEFAN and REBECCA kiss. Music ends.

STEFAN Goodnight, Miss Almazoff.

REBECCA Goodnight, Mr. Dudar.

They exit into their houses. MIKE arrives home, still in his work clothes, looking exhausted and careworn. At the same time, Captain McDOUGALL approaches the house. MIKE sees him and hurries to steer him away.

MIKE Not here!

McDOUGALL Looks like you get the whole fifty, Sokolowski.

MIKE Quiet, for Chrissakes!

McDOUGALL   As soon as we've made the arrest.

MIKE   I need it now! I told you—

McDOUGALL   And I need that name. Believe me, you don't want to start withholding evidence.

MIKE   Do you have children?

McDOUGALL   That's none of your business.

MIKE   Is there an army of Bolsheviks marching toward their doorstep? Captain, four tickets to Canada cost four hundred dollars. I need the last fifty, and I need it now.

McDOUGALL   You're going to have to trust me.

MIKE   *(pause)* The man you're looking for is the Jewish journalist. Moishe Almazoff.

McDOUGALL   You'll get the money the minute we pick him up. One honest man to another.

> *MIKE exits to his house, McDOUGALL to the street.*

ACT ONE   Scene Nine

> *Ashdown mansion, South Winnipeg, early the next morning.*
>
> *SUSAN ASHDOWN nervously looks out the window. EMMA the maid stands nearby.*

SUSAN   It's deathly quiet. No cars. I don't think I've seen a soul out this window all day.

EMMA   Ma'am?

SUSAN   *(not paying attention)* I just pray it ends quickly, for everyone's sake.

EMMA   Ma'am?

SUSAN   Yes, Emma.

EMMA   You and the mister – you've been good as saints, taking pity on me after me husband's loss.

SUSAN   Of course.

EMMA   Especially with me mouth shootin' off all the time, God bless yas. But I've been thinking about it and—

SUSAN   You're not thinking of going out?

EMMA   I'm not wanting you to think I'm ungrateful—

SUSAN   You have to think of your child.

EMMA   It is me Joey I am thinking about, ma'am. Sure we don't have a pot to piss in, but he's gotta know what's right. Joey'll see his mother can stand up for something just as well as any man.

> *JAMES ASHDOWN enters.*

JAMES   Well, there's our mayor for you. Law and order, all huff and puff. Says the first signs of radical elements, he'll smash them immediately. The twit.

SUSAN   This whole thing reminds me of that horrible business with Riel.

JAMES   Nothing to fear, love. I told him myself, the workers will blow off a bit of steam and the whole thing will resolve itself.

SUSAN   I think it's more than that.

JAMES   *(looking from SUSAN to EMMA)* Red Emma has been in touch with the Kremlin, has she? Don't worry, love. The volunteer committee will curb the Bolsheviks. The lights will shine and the water flow.

SUSAN   Listen, James. It could get much worse than we've thought—

JAMES   Senator Robertson will handle it. He is appointed by the prime minister himself—

> *From the street, a menacing chant starts up.*

STRIKERS   Strike while the iron's hot
Get what we haven't got... *(repeatedly)*

> *The ASHDOWNS freeze, convinced by the tone of the marchers that revolution is at their door. JAMES goes to a nearby cabinet drawer and pulls out a revolver.*
>
> *The marchers near the house, the menace of the chant building. JAMES points the gun towards the marchers.*

SUSAN   James, stop it!

> *A loud bang makes them snap their attention stage right. SUSAN shrieks.*

JAMES   *(shouting)* Stay away I tell you.

SUSAN   Oh my God! It was a bird James!

JAMES   What? What do you—

SUSAN   A bird! A bird! A bird flew into the window!

JAMES   *(barely paying attention, gun still pointed)* Get Senator Robertson on the telephone.

>   *SUSAN runs over to the telephone. She looks at EMMA, still standing in the same position.*

SUSAN   Go!

EMMA   Yes, ma'am.

>   *EMMA slips out without JAMES noticing. SUSAN taps the phone receiver, repeatedly.*

SUSAN   The lines are dead.

>   *Blackout.*

ACT ONE   Scene Ten

>   *The downtown streets, immediately after.*
>
>   *Music begins. [Play CD Track #10 – "Strike!"]*
>
>   *Workers throughout the city triumphantly march to the city's centre.*

ALL

>   Strike while the iron's hot to
>   Get what we haven't got and
>   Take back the things they took and
>   Make right the wrongs and look right
>   Into their eyes until they
>   Blink realizin' that we
>   Won't give up the fight no so
>   Muster up your might and
>   Strike!

>   *A UNION REP addresses the crowd.*

UNION REP   May 15th, 1919 will go down in history as the day that the workers of Winnipeg, Canada stood united with the workers of the world!

>   *Militant shouts of approval.*

We have withdrawn labour from all industry, and withdrawn we will stay until the bosses realize that they cannot stand against our masses!

More shouts of approval. MOISHE steps forward into the crowd where he embraces REBECCA and STEFAN. McCREADY is close by as bodyguard.

ALL   *(singing)* No telephones!
                      No telegrams!
                      No posties
                      Taxies
                      Barbers
                      Streetcars
                      Metal trades
                      No kitchen maids
                      No hired aids
                      No papers
                      Painters
                      Bakers
                      Waiters
                      Unionized
                      Or otherwise
                      Temporaries
                      Full-time labour
                      They all heed the call and

                      Strike while the iron's hot to
                      Get what we haven't got and
                      Take back the things they took and
                      Make right the wrongs and look right
                      Into their eyes until they
                      Blink realizin' that we
                      Won't give up the fight no so
                      Muster up your might and
                      Strike!

McDOUGALL steps in, watching the crowd. McCREADY sees him.

McCREADY   Stefan, police that way, come on.

STEFAN, REBECCA follow McCREADY's lead, leaving MOISHE as they disappear into the crowd. Senator ROBERTSON enters.

ROBERTSON   *(staring at the crowd)* Good God.

McDOUGALL   *(approaching)* We'd need an army to control this lot. And, sir? That man is your letter writer, Moishe Almazoff.

ROBERTSON   Then bloody well grab him.

McDOUGALL   Hasn't broken any laws and he's got citizenship.

ROBERTSON   Every last strike leader's hiding behind a British passport.

McDOUGALL   Brits? We can't touch 'em.

ROBERTSON   Start recruiting your army. I'll take care of the law and you be damn well ready to enforce it.

McDOUGALL   Aye. Sir.

> *ROBERTSON exits. McDOUGALL begins exiting in the opposite direction, sees O'REILLY at the edge of the strikers.*

O'Reilly! If you're still wanting a job, get to the station fast and pick up a uniform.

> *McDOUGALL exits. O'REILLY watches him go, looks from McDOUGALL to the strikers.*

O'REILLY   *(to himself)* No thank you, sir.

> *He steps in with the strikers.*

WORKERS   *(singing)* Strike while the iron's hot
Get what we haven't got
Strike while the iron's hot
Get what we haven't got
Strike while the iron's hot
Get what we haven't got
Strike while the iron's hot
Get what we haven't got

ALL   No firemen
No hired men
No porters
Sorters
Teamsters
Seamsters
Carpenters
No caretakers   .
No bricklayers
No printers
Tinsmiths
Janitors
Elevators
Unionized
Or otherwise
Twenty thousand

Thirty thousand
Shut this city down and

Strike while the iron's hot to
Get what we haven't got and
Take back the things they took and
Make right the wrongs and look right
Into their eyes until they
Blink realizin' that we
Won't give up the fight no so
Muster up your might and

Strike while the iron's hot to
Get what we haven't got and...

The sound of the strikers fades down.

STEFAN and REBECCA emerge at the far end of the crowd.

REBECCA   The whole world will be watching this.

MIKE enters, looking for STEFAN.

STEFAN   Six thousand people they're saying!

ANOTHER STRIKER   I say eight thousand!

They see MIKE.

STEFAN   Mike! Look at this! You still think things cannot change?

MIKE   Read this to me.

STEFAN takes a letter from MIKE.

STEFAN   *(delighted)* From Anna!

MIKE   No.

STEFAN   *(checking the signature)* Peh-TROH BEE-lee?

MIKE   The neighbour.

STEFAN   *(reading the salutation in Ukrainian)* "Do-ro-HEY Mich- EYE-loh..."

STEFAN reads, scanning and summarizing for MIKE.

"Bol-she-VEH-keh veez-MEH-leh oo-KREYE-yee-nah. Anna poh-MAHRR-leh." [*Ukrainian: The Bolsheviks have taken Ukraine. Your Anna has been killed.*]

Beat.

REBECCA   What is it?

MIKE   Ah DYEE-teh? *[Ukrainian: And the children?]*

STEFAN   Demyan… Taras… Tekla… fshee poh-MAHRR-leh. *[Ukrainian: All dead.]*

MIKE   Fshee? *[Ukrainian: All of them?]*

> *STEFAN nods.*

STEFAN   Mike…

> *STEFAN moves to touch MIKE. MIKE's arm jumps, violently hitting STEFAN's hand away.*

Mike?

> *MIKE stumbles away.*

REBECCA   Stefan, what?

STEFAN · The Russians have invaded Kiev. Ten thousand killed.

REBECCA   Anna and the children?

STEFAN   All dead.

> *MIKE has disappeared into the crowd.*

Mike!

> *STEFAN follows where MIKE disappeared.*

STRIKERS   *(singing)* Strike while the iron's hot to
                    Get what we haven't got and
                    Take back the things they took and
                    Make right the wrongs and look right
                    Into their eyes until they
                    Blink realizin' that we
                    Won't give up the fight no so
                    Muster up your might and
                    Strike!!!

> *Music ends. Act One curtain.*

Full Cast
Photo by Andrew Sikorsky

ACT TWO   Scene One

City Hall, the next day.

Entr'acte music begins. [Play CD Track #11 – "A City Shut Down Instrumental."]

The city is shut tight. McDOUGALL enters as a SHOPKEEPER changes a store window sign from "Open" to "On Strike."

A PEDDLER pushes on his cart. McDOUGALL is about to stop him, but the PEDDLER displays a "Permitted by Order of the Strike Committee." McDOUGALL gives him the all clear, and exits.

A crowd of strikers begins to gather. STEFAN walks among them, showing a photograph. People shake their heads, no – they haven't seen MIKE.

Entr'acte music ends. New music begins. [Allow CD to continue playing through to Track #12 – "Ultimatum."]

STEFAN joins REBECCA within the crowd in front of City Hall. WALLACE and O'REILLY are close to STEFAN.

CROWD   Hear us out! Hear us out!

Senator ROBERTSON comes out of City Hall, addresses the mob.

ROBERTSON   I will not be provoked. The motive behind this strike is clearly the overthrow of constitutional government.

A UNION REPRESENTATIVE jumps up on the steps.

UNION REP   (*singing*) He won't meet us
                      He won't speak t'us
                      He'll just improvise invective
                      Posturing with yammering
                      'Bout quelling rebellious
                      Activity

ROBERTSON   I don't bargain
                      I won't pardon
                      I won't recognize collective
                      Bargaining as anything
                      But tampering with governing
                      Authority

ALL & ROBERTSON
                      Ultimatum

My [His] words verbatim
Debate them
Mistake them? Best ye [we] not
Ultimatum
Your [Our] jobs: vacate them
Negate them
Erase them, pensions gone

Ultimatum
Your [Our] hopes, I'll [he'll] break them
Deflate them
Replacements take your [our] jobs

The crowd screams insults at ROBERTSON.

ROBERTSON   Disperse yourselves immediately. I will not bargain
with a mob. The government of Canada will not give in to the threat of
a general strike.

You must yield first
Sign this deal first
This takes force immediately by
Severing your unioning,
Eliminating striking but
You'll have jobs

UNION REP   There's no parting
From our starving
But he wounds our dignity with
Patronizing, taxing lies
Impeding us and feeding us straight
To the dogs

ALL& ROBERTSON

Ultimatum
My [His] words verbatim
Debate them
Mistake them? Best ye [we] not
Ultimatum
Your [Our] jobs: vacate them
Negate them
Erase them, pensions gone

Ultimatum
Your [Our] hopes, I'll [he'll] break them
Deflate them
Replacements take your [our] jobs

ROBERTSON exits. The strikers' solidarity is at a fever pitch and the whole group is in no mood for compromise.

SUFFRAGETTE *(shouting)* Senator Robertson and the Citizens Committee demand we go back to work at 10:00 a.m. tomorrow! What do we say to that?

STRIKERS *(shouting with defiant fists in air)* NO!!!

SUFFRAGETTE And they demand we end our union affiliation—

STRIKERS NO!!!

SUFFRAGETTE And they demand we never take part in a General Strike again—

STRIKERS NO!!! NO!!! NO!!!

ALL   Ultimatum
                       Our hopes – can't take 'em
                       Or break 'em
                       Forsake them we will not

l to r: Marc Devigne, Leora Joy Godden, Tim Hildebrand, Mark Oddan, Carol Wylie, Bruce McKay, Jeff Pufahl, Deborah Buck
Photo by Jody Longworth

Music ends. Captain McDOUGALL enters. WALLACE and O'REILLY, now acting as STEFAN's bodyguards, pull STEFAN and REBECCA away.

ACT TWO   Scene Two

Sokolowski / Almazoff house. Three days later.

STEFAN and REBECCA enter from opposite sides of the street. WALLACE follows, a respectful distance from STEFAN, but O'REILLY arrives to take up the watch post, and WALLACE exits.

REBECCA   Still no sign?

STEFAN   Four days is long. Usually he drinks, I know where he is. I've never been this long without him. Not since we left Ukraine.

MOISHE   *(entering)* He's not in Point Douglas. None of the madams have seen him.

REBECCA   He'll be okay. Days are getting warmer.

STEFAN   Nights are still cold.

MOISHE   Don't worry, Stefan. He has a reason to take care of himself.

STEFAN   Like what?

REBECCA   Are you kidding? He looks at you the same way our Tah-teh looked at us. He'll be back.

STEFAN   Yeah, yeah.

REBECCA   And summer will come soon.

MOISHE   And we will win the strike.

STEFAN   If it doesn't go on a year.

REBECCA   Then we will march for a year.

STEFAN   If it doesn't go on three years.

MOISHE   We will march for three years.

STEFAN   If we don't starve first.

REBECCA   I know many, many ways to cook potatoes.

STEFAN   Except we aren't making any difference.

O'REILLY   None 'a my business but joining this strike was the farthest ting from my mind. I can't say I so much as ever talked to Jewish folks before either. And that Orangeman from the Union just now – I can guarantee he never had a good ting to say about a Catholic in his whole life. I'm just saying, if you think you're not makin' a difference – I'd call ya wrong.

REBECCA   There. Mike will be back. And we will change the world.

STEFAN   Yeah yeah.

REBECCA   Yeah yeah. Thousands showing up in Victoria Park.

MOISHE   And sympathy strikes in Vancouver, Calgary, Toronto.

REBECCA   Not too bad, Stefan Dudar.

STEFAN   It's a start, Rebecca Almazoff.

REBECCA   The world is up for grabs, and we are shaping it new.

> *Music begins. [Play CD Track #13 – "Better Days."]*
>
>> *(singing)* Better the days
>> More modern the ways
>> The past is so hazy
>> The future so clearly shaped
>> Out with the old and
>> "Hello" to the very new
>> We can all look forward to
>> Better days

STEFAN   No. For all we know, Mike may be already deported. They could deport any of us tomorrow. All of us.

MOISHE   *(imitating a pompous bureaucrat)* Mister Duh-dar, is it? We have deported Mister Ska-wow-ski for the crime of being Ukrainian.

REBECCA   And we have decided to deport you, well, just because!

MOISHE   If you sneeze

REBECCA   Deport him

MOISHE   Dirty knees

REBECCA   Deport him

MOISHE   Didn't say "Please"

REBECCA   Deportable sleaze
                       Stung by bees

MOISHE	Deport him
REBECCA	Late with fees
MOISHE	Deport him *(miming urinating)* Watered some trees
STEFAN	*(holding his hand in front of his mouth)* Deportable disease

REBECCA, MOISHE & STEFAN   *(pointing at one another and holding their noses)*
Deport him [her] oh do, please

REBECCA   When the strike ends, we'll all buy houses on Wellington Crescent.

STEFAN   Good, 'cause I don't have a red penny for the rent and I'm sick of potatoes.

REBECCA   Better the days
So hopeful this place

l to r: Dana Horrox, Cherise Kotelniski, Catherine Wreford, Tyson Wiebe, Sharon Bajer, David Friedman, Taras Luchak, Marc Devigne, Jeffrey Kohut, Matt Kippen
Photo by Andrew Sikorsky

> The moon in new phase the
> Horizon so freshly painted
> Better tomorrows
> Not hoarded by oh so few
> Every soul is destined to
> Better days
> Better days
> We are all so surely due
> Better days

STEFAN *(imitating MOISHE's bureaucrat voice)* We see, uh, Mr. Al-mo-zoff, that you are a follower of Karl Marx—

MOISHE Yes. Every day I follow him home on the Dufferin Avenue trolley.

O'REILLY Ha! Fell into our trap. Everyone knows there's no trolley on Dufferin.

> *O'REILLY comes over to join in.*

STEFAN	*(singing)* If he breathes
MALE GROUP	Deport him
STEFAN	If he bleeds
MALE GROUP	Deport him
STEFAN	Can't speak with ease
REBECCA	Deporting's a breeze No good spleen
MALE GROUP	Deport him
REBECCA	Ends with "ski"
MALE GROUP	Deport him
STEFAN	Garlic-smelling meals
MALE GROUP	*(shrugging)* Deport him with his peels
ALL	Deport me someone, please

O'REILLY Now everybody just calm down and don't get yer delicates in a knot. 'Cause if anyone from the Immigration Department dares show his face around here, he's gonna have to deal with me first.

MOISHE Oh, really?

O'REILLY No. O'Reilly.

ALL   Better the days
Secure in our fate
Our hearts will be blazing
Our minds in a peaceful state
Freed from our sorrows
And soaring on happy tunes
There'll be more than just a few
Better days
Better days
We are all so surely due
Better days

No one notices MIKE has entered from the opposite end of the street and is watching the conclusion of the song.

There'll be more than just a few
Better days
Better days
We are all so surely due
Better days

Music ends. MIKE applauds cheerfully.

MIKE   Are you dancing on my grave or is everyone a Jew now?

STEFAN   Mike!

REBECCA   You're back!

MOISHE   Thank God, you're safe!

STEFAN runs to MIKE and embraces him. O'REILLY retreats to his guard position on the edge of the group.

STEFAN   Mike.... Where the hell have you been?

MIKE   Christ spent forty days in the desert. Four days in Vin-ni-pag is about the same.

REBECCA   We were very troubled to hear about your family, Mister Sokolowski.

MIKE   You should be troubled it was Jews that killed my family.

STEFAN   Mike, these are our neighbours.

MIKE   A Jewish Bohl-sheh-veh-kee army.

MOISHE   We are conscripted, the same as—

MIKE   Followers of Karl Marx. Jew.

MOISHE   The same as Ukrainians are conscripted—

MIKE   Led by Leon Trotsky. Jew.

STEFAN   Mike, stop it.

MOISHE   *(overlapping)* The Russian Army is about as Jewish as the Pope.

MIKE   *(overlapping)* I are not interested in your propaganda.

MOISHE   Ee-DEH doh CHORT! *[Ukrainian: Go to the Devil!]*

> *MOISHE exits.*

MIKE   *(calling after him)* Thanks to your strike, the government cracks down on enemy aliens. You watch. They will start with big political writers.

> *O'REILLY retreats a respectful distance from the family scene.*

REBECCA   Moishe and I are Canadian citizens.

MIKE   You think you are safe from the government? They don't like a law, they change it. Anyone born outside this country can now be deported. Any time.

REBECCA   How do you know this?

MIKE   It is amazing what people will talk about when they step over a drunk.

REBECCA   If the government calls us enemies, it only makes us better friends. Don't fight us, Mr. Sokolowski. Join us.

MIKE   Stay away from my godson!

STEFAN   Mike, stop this now!

REBECCA   Mr. Sokolowski, you are not the only one ever to lose family in Ukraine.

> *REBECCA exits. O'REILLY exits.*

STEFAN   They are my friends—

MIKE   You listen now—

STEFAN   You are not my father!

MIKE   I am your godfather!

STEFAN   I love her.

> *MIKE slaps him.*

MIKE   My family would be alive today. Your parents would be alive. If the Jew had loaned them the money.

STEFAN   They would all be alive. If you had not called the moneylender a filthy lying Shylock, they would all be here with us.

> *STEFAN follows REBECCA's exit.*

ACT TWO   Scene Three

> *Central Police Station, a few days later.*

> *Senator ROBERTSON enters, followed by Captain McDOUGALL.*

McDOUGALL   What in the hell are you thinking?

ROBERTSON   Captain McDougall, I believe you're out of order.

McDOUGALL   All this time the strike's been going on and not a whiff of trouble, and that's because every man on the force is out there each and every day.

ROBERTSON   Yes, Captain, but a nice, peaceful, lengthy strike is not what is required.

> *Music Begins. [Play CD Track #14 – "Desperate Times."]*

McDOUGALL   If upholding the peace is not required, then what in God's name is?

ROBERTSON   A police force I can trust.

> (*singing*) Desperate times
> Desperate measures
> Those in league with the Devil
> Would lead us and feed us
> Deceitful and dastardly lies
> No surprise
>
> Desperate times
> Desperate measures
> Iron rule gives no pleasure (*picking up a billy club*)
> But see this and heed this, believe me
> Such sinister minds
> I won't abide

> *Music continues as underscore.*

McDOUGALL   I'd bust the head of me own brother, I would, if the upholding of the rightful law was at stake.

ROBERTSON   Good. Because every man on the force can either forego his right to strike or hand in his badge.

McDOUGALL   Then you'll be wanting this.

> *He takes off his badge, lays it on the desk. ROBERTSON leaves the station, McDOUGALL remains. POLICE OFFICERS enter the station, removing their badges and leaving.*
>
> *At the same time, ROBERTSON runs straight into JAMES and SUSAN ASHDOWN who have been hurrying to the station.*

JAMES   Gideon, we've just heard—

SUSAN   *(riding over top of him)* We have just heard an unbelievable rumour.

ROBERTSON   If it's regarding your police, yes.

SUSAN   You've fired the entire force?

ROBERTSON   The police are just another union, hand in hand with the strikers. It had to be done.

SUSAN   You asked us to support law and order, not insanity!

JAMES
>Desperate times
>Desperate measures
>Still our heads must be level
>Or dealings and feelings and
>Reason and sanity die
>We must try

SUSAN
>Surely to God there must be something more reasonable
>Legal dissent is hardly so treasonable
>I can't believe that bargaining's not feasible
>This we'll surely regret

> *As ROBERTSON speaks, a new group of men line up and take up the badges the police officers had turned in, and are assigned wooden clubs. These are the new Special Police Force – SPECIALS.*

ROBERTSON   If I'm to regain control, I require loyalty. I've assembled a Special Police Force made entirely of British veterans.

SUSAN   Soldiers are trained in fighting, not in peace! Gideon, you've completely botched the whole situation. You've turned a strike into a war.

ROBERTSON   And need I remind you, ma'am, we are under the provisions of the War Measures Act? I have the full authority to do whatever I must.

SUSAN   And how far will you go?

ROBERTSON   Just watch me.

> Surely to God we have evidence so plausible
> Revolt at our door we see is now probable
> The strongest of measures, or else we are vulnerable
> Need we more to convince?

ROBERTSON & ASHDOWNS

> Desperate times
> Desperate measures
> Now we all test our mettle
> And pray that one day in our graves
> We won't ridiculed be
> For now we see
> Desperate times
> Desperate measures
> Desperate times
> Desperate measures

Music ends. ROBERTSON and the ASHDOWNS exit. Captain McDOUGALL remains in the Police Station. He is covering framed photos of officers—the department's "Wall of Honour"—with black cloth. O'REILLY enters.

O'REILLY   I heard the news, sir. I'm sorry.

McDOUGALL   Remember McKee, O'Reilly?

O'REILLY   Sure.

McDOUGALL   How valiantly 'e fought? How nobly 'e fell? *(covering the photo)* This city's done a grievous injury to the memory of our war dead, these here police boys.

O'REILLY   I go over it all and wonder sometimes just what the hell we were doing over there. *(a short pause)* 'Member Christmas in '14?

McDOUGALL   I still canna believe they called a truce.

O'REILLY   Krauts exchanging gifts and trink with us. And that Fritz wit the singin' voice.

McDOUGALL   'E sung "Tipperary" sweet as a lark.

O'REILLY *(smiling)* English better 'n yours, I'll offer.

They chuckle, but then O'REILLY turns serious.

Right nears the end, when we was pushin' 'em back… I 'ad a Kraut holed up in his lair. I 'ad my bayonet right at 'is heart, ready to finish 'im off…. And 'e knows it's 'is last breaths 'e's breathin'. And sure as Christ 'e starts singin' Tipperary.

McDOUGALL The same Fritz?

O'REILLY One and the same.

McDOUGALL Wad ya do?

O'REILLY I could'na do it. I kicked 'im good in the arse and sent 'im home to 'is wife and children.

McDOUGALL Ya shoulda pierced the bastard.

O'REILLY Nah. He was no more the enemy than you're a saint.

McDOUGALL That's a load of codswallop.

O'REILLY Tink of it, sir. We've got more in common with the Fritz on McGregor Avenue than the Brit on Wellington Crescent.

McDOUGALL No. No. What of these boys?

He points to the Wall of Honour.

All of 'em dead at the hands of the Fritz.

O'REILLY These boys were sold a bag o' beans just like you and I, and you know it. And when it comes right down to it, we're all jus' waitin' for the sniper.

Music begins. [Play CD Track #15 – "O'Reilly's Song."]

McDOUGALL Ah, I'll give you that one. But we was killin' 'em not six months ago—

O'REILLY Well I won't be killing 'em again.

> Red was the blood of the men I've slain
> Brown was the mud in the trenches where they lay
> And black is the heart when the truth of war's made
>   plain:
>
> Death has a way of making every man the same
>
> Green was the grass when the war began
> Blue was the sky 'til the smokin' of the cannon

> And grey is the world where the honest 'ting don't
> happen
> But history reeks of such wrongs we canna fathom
>
> And fall though I, a small man such as I
> I'll rise again where King's armies have fallen

McDOUGALL & O'REILLY
> Red was the blood of the men I've slain
> Brown was the mud in the trenches where they lay
> But black is the heart when the truth of war's made
> plain:
> Death has a way of making every man the same

O'REILLY
> Black is me heart 'til that dreaded judgement day
> If I gets to live, I've many debts to pay

Music ends.

We could use your help, sir. We really could.

McDOUGALL opens a drawer in his desk.

McDOUGALL   One last bit of police business.

He pulls out a small leather sack.

ACT TWO   Scene Four

Near the Sokolowski / Almazoff house. Later that evening.

*REBECCA and STEFAN walking home. A BODYGUARD follows
them. STEFAN indicates they're okay from here. The BODYGUARD
exits.*

STEFAN   I have learned some things, Rebecca Almazoff.

REBECCA   What have you learned?

STEFAN   I have learned that your eyes shine blue in the morning, a little
bit grey in the afternoon, and almost green in the evening. I have learned
that you can argue better than anyone, including your famous brother.
I have learned that what I used to think was all simple—that there's one
side and the other side—I don't think that so much anymore. And I have
learned that you can buy almost anything from a Jewish peddler.

He gives her a small box wrapped in shiny paper.

REBECCA   What is it?

STEFAN   Come on.

REBECCA   *(unwrapping it)* Chocolate!

STEFAN   I bought it before the strike. And then... with Mike gone... the time wasn't right. The time isn't right now either...

REBECCA   No, the time is fine...

STEFAN   No, because I can't afford to buy you chocolate any more. And I can't afford a ring. Even if the shops weren't closed up...

REBECCA   Are you... proposing?

STEFAN   I am trying not to, because I know you don't want me to—

REBECCA   Stefan...

STEFAN   But listen. It wouldn't have to be a Catholic marriage, or a Jewish marriage, or even any marriage at all... if we could just be together.

> *For a moment, she does not answer.*

REBECCA   I have learned some things as well, Stefan Dudar. And I have been thinking that maybe what I thought was complicated before, isn't maybe so much.

STEFAN   Yes?

CARMICHAEL   *(offstage)* This is the place.

> *BODYGUARD runs back on.*

BODYGUARD   *(to STEFAN)* Get in the house!

> *CARMICHAEL and three others approach carrying clubs, all dressed as civilians except wearing white arm bands that identify them as newly-hired SPECIALS.*
>
> *Hearing the noise, MIKE steps out to the porch.*

STEFAN   *(to REBECCA)* They've come for me.

BODYGUARD   Get in the house!

CARMICHAEL   Shut him up!

> *A SPECIAL beats the BODYGUARD.*

REBECCA   Why are you here?

STEFAN   *(overlapping)* Rebecca, get inside!

REBECCA *(overlapping)* You have no business here!

MOISHE comes out onto the porch.

SPECIAL #1 Where is he?

REBECCA Where is who?

CARMICHAEL *(accusing STEFAN)* Moishe Almazoff?

SPECIAL #2 *(overlapping)* Is that him?

MOISHE I am Moishe Almazoff.

CARMICHAEL Get him.

REBECCA Moishe!

Two SPECIALS grab MOISHE on the porch.

MOISHE Take it easy!

STEFAN *(overlapping)* He's done nothing wrong!

REBECCA *(overlapping)* You have no right to do this!

SPECIAL #3 Stand up!

MOISHE What is my charge?

REBECCA Get your hands off him! He is a citizen!

MOISHE *(overlapping)* You have a warrant? Show me!

STEFAN What is his charge?

SPECIAL #1 Shut up!

SPECIAL #1 hits MOISHE with his club.

CARMICHAEL How about conspiracy to overthrow the Government of the Dominion of Canada?

Music begins. [Play CD Track #16 – "Kiss Him Goodbye."]

> So you can
> Kiss him goodbye
> Pretend he's dead and gone
> Cause from here on he's
> Deemed deportable
> Alien

MIKE watches as CARMICHAEL handcuffs MOISHE, while STEFAN and REBECCA are held back by two SPECIALS.

l to r: Tyson Wiebe, Jeffrey Kohut, David Friedman (kneeling),
Jay Brazeau, Kevin Aichele
Photo by Andrew Sikorsky

REBECCA   I can't lose him—

STEFAN   You won't—

REBECCA   He is all my family—

STEFAN   We'll get him out—

MOISHE, REBECCA, STEFAN
Don't kiss me [him] goodbye
I'll [he'll] be back by dawn
This is far too wrong
Clearly laughable
Goings on

CARMICHAEL, SPECIALS
So kiss him goodbye
Pretend he's dead and gone
'Cause from here on he's
Deemed deportable
Alien

McDOUGALL enters in street clothes as the SPECIALS drag MOISHE off.

CARMICHAEL *(exiting)* Thirteen to go, lads!

MIKE sees McDOUGALL, hurries over to him.

McDOUGALL Sokolowski.

MIKE Get out.

McDOUGALL holds out the small leather bag from the Police Station.

McDOUGALL I gave you my word.

MIKE I don't want it any more.

McDOUGALL Lord help you, Sokolowski. Where the hell do you stand?

McDOUGALL drops the bag of silver on the ground.

STEFAN Mike. You?

McDOUGALL You asked about my family. One boy I've got. He's seven. One honest man to another.

McDOUGALL exits.

MIKE *(to STEFAN)* I had no choice.

STEFAN For money?

MIKE For Anna, the children...

STEFAN They're dead!

REBECCA walks fast in the direction of the soldiers.

Rebecca.

REBECCA *(furious)* Do not follow me.

STEFAN I will confess. They'll let him go.

REBECCA And so will I and we will both be deported.

STEFAN It has to be me.

REBECCA I need to be with my own.

STEFAN I'll come with you.

REBECCA No! You won't.

REBECCA runs off.

MIKE ` Stefan…. If they didn't come for him…. It would have been you.

STEFAN turns on MIKE.

STEFAN (*singing*) This is goodbye
Don't come near me I
Know so clearly why
Here this day for me
You have died

STEFAN exits after REBECCA.

Music ends. [Allow CD Track #16 to continue playing to CD Track #17 – One Heart at a Time.]

ACT TWO   Scene Five

A street nearby, immediately after.

REBECCA ALMAZOFF enters, still furious.

REBECCA (*singing*) Lives destroyed in a flash
When the knives of the tribes seek a clash
The battles of old
Are retold so the grievances last
And I'd be the first
To avenge the worst
Of wrongs of the past
I have to tell myself that

Worlds change one heart at a time
Empires fall when just one soldier leaves the line
Even love finds one heart at a time
Hearts can change but can change start in mine?

I'm as guilty as those
Whose ancient disputes come to blows
But what would I prove
With a move that would lash out at foes?
My fist wants to try
"An eye for an eye"
But reason begs me to slow
I can only pray that

STEFAN enters, listens.

> Worlds change one heart at a time
> Empires fall when just one soldier leaves the line
> Even love finds one heart at a time
> Hearts can change but can change start in mine?

STEFAN   Change will come. It has to.

REBECCA   You think it's so easy. It isn't. I want to kill him.

STEFAN   Mike's hatred is old. It belongs to the Old Country. It's not ours.

REBECCA   It is mine. I feel it.

STEFAN   I know you, Rebecca Almazoff. You heart is big enough to make room for something else.

> (*singing*) Old wisdom has shown
> We should be foes
> There are those who now say that we're
> Crazed, out of our minds
> And they're right
> But such foolishness might make the

STEFAN & REBECCA

> World change one heart at a time
> Empires fall when just one soldier leaves the line
> Even love finds one heart at a time
> Hearts can change and the change starts with mine

REBECCA   Those men said thirteen more – they're arresting all the strike leaders. We have to go to the Labour Temple.

STEFAN   No – first the Legion Hall.

REBECCA   There's only veterans there.

STEFAN   We have far more friends than you know.

They exit. Music ends.

ACT TWO   Scene Six

Senator ROBERTSON's suite, the Royal Alexandra Hotel, next day.

The suite is presidential. ROBERTSON is seated at a heavy dark wood writing table. He speaks to an offstage bellboy.

ROBERTSON *(annoyed but keeping his cool)* Please tell them I cannot meet with them—

>   Corporal O'REILLY and Captain McDOUGALL enter, caps in hand.

McDougall! You're not an official delegation.

O'REILLY A thousand apologies Senator, sir. Corporal Sean O'Reilly, discharged. Consider us a wee delegation of two. The two wise men, as it were. *(breaking the ice)* And one of us wiser than the other.

>   McDOUGALL smiles but ROBERTSON is unamused.

ROBERTSON Gentlemen. I am dealing with a potential national disaster. Your frivolity, and your presence are unwelcome.

O'REILLY And I can assure you, Senator, the nature of our visit is entirely un-frivolous.

McDOUGALL *(impatiently)* It's about Moishe Almazoff and the others, sir—

ROBERTSON *(curtly)* He's in prison, awaiting due process with the rest of the foreigners.

McDOUGALL Senator Robertson, sir. I'd be the first ta tell you. I'm no lover of the immigrant. But the man's no riff-raff. He helped returned soldiers with the flu and stuck it out even though his own father was dying of it.

ROBERTSON *(matter-of-factly)* The net widely cast ensnares some unfortunate species. Good day.

O'REILLY Sir, you might be aware quite a few of the returned lads have come round to sympathizing with the strike. If you could speak with them, it might calm things considerable before the big march tomorrow.

ROBERTSON Then inform them that as of *1:00 p.m.* today, all public gathering in this city for the purpose of demonstration has been outlawed.

McDOUGALL Ya can't deny simple free speech!

ROBERTSON I will enforce the law and the will of the government. Anybody that gathers to demonstrate after today will be arrested.

O'REILLY Oh, there'll be a fair number of 'em, sir.

ROBERTSON And they'll meet one thousand Special Police and the same number of military.

McDOUGALL To put down a peaceful demonstration?

O'REILLY   Sir, I have to beg you. Don't loose the Specials on this march. There's returned soldiers on both sides – and the tempers are bound for boilin'.

ROBERTSON   Breaking the law will be taken as provocation.

O'REILLY   I've seen the men on both sides, and there's many a loose cannon among them and more than a one with the shell-shock besides—

ROBERTSON   Let the chips fall where they may.

McDOUGALL   (*incredulous*) You're washin' your 'ands of it?

ROBERTSON   My hands, and conscience, are clean, sir.

He raises his hand, indicating they should head to the door.

Gentlemen.

O'REILLY   Well that's that then.

He turns to exit but then stops.

You know lads, I'm no gem in the crown of Ireland, and me mother, she always said me impertinence was one of me more endearing charms. So, if you'll not speak with the soldiers, Senator, permit me to make me dear mother proud and read you the following.

ROBERTSON   Read me what?

O'REILLY quickly pulls out a written statement.

O'REILLY   "We state with regret that by your dogged pursuit of certain foreigners within our midst, and the shameful manner of their arrest, and their continued persecution under the guise of the law, you have proven yourself in opposition to the true spirit of Democracy which we, the returned soldiers, fought for on the fields of Flanders." (*pause*) There. That's what the boys woulda said to you, sir.

O'REILLY taps McDOUGALL on the arm to exit, but McDOUGALL hesitates.

McDOUGALL   In case you missed the lad's sentiment, I'd like to add: You can kiss me arse.

They exit.

ACT TWO   Scene Seven

Sokolowski / Almazoff house, the next morning.

From the ALMAZOFF house, REBECCA steps out onto the porch. She takes a moment to weigh her strength for facing the day. STEFAN steps out behind her. A pause. He puts his arm around her waist.

REBECCA   Are you ready for this?

STEFAN   This beautiful morning? I think I'm ready for anything.

> *They kiss, but are interrupted as MIKE enters from his apartment, duffle bag in hand. REBECCA sees him and retreats to her house.*

I have nothing to say to you.

MIKE   *(pause)* I am going back to the farm. Where we first worked. You were very young. I can draw a map if you can't remember how to find it.

STEFAN   Sure.

MIKE   Only fourteen. You worked like a grown man, after a while. Look at you now. Strong like bull, smart like… ah, you know. *(pause)* If there are children… your parents would have wanted them to be raised Catholic.

STEFAN   Jesus, Mike…

MIKE   And the wedding. I would like to know.

STEFAN   Mike, you put Rebecca's brother in jail. And you talk about family.

MIKE   Yes.

> *Resigned, MIKE begins to exit.*

STEFAN   Then first do this.

> *MIKE stops.*

March with us to free him.

MIKE   They have made marching illegal.

STEFAN   Demonstration is illegal. We won't demonstrate. We are not holding signs or shouting. We won't break their laws. We will march in silence.

MIKE   They will arrest you.

STEFAN   Then it will be a very crowded jail.

MIKE   Have you seen Main Street? Soldiers everywhere. Mounted Police. City Hall is surrounded by Gatling guns! Stefan, don't do this!

STEFAN   Mike, we have to. You have to.

Music begins. [Play CD Track #18 – "Do It For Anna."]

> (*singing*) You wouldn't do it for your godson
> Nor a woman who's a Jew
> You wouldn't do it for her brother
> Who you wrongfully accused
> You won't even do it for your God who you
> Don't worship anymore
> But I know deep down what moved you to do
> All you did before
>
> You'd do it for Anna
> You'd do it for Demyan
> You'd do it for Tekla and Taras
> You'd join in a chorus and march to the ends of the
> earth
> You'd do it for Anna
> For your little fam'ly
> So what has happened to them
> Never happens again
> Let their lives multiply in their worth
> Do it for Anna
> Do it for Demyan
> Do it for Tekla
> Do it for Taras
> Make your amends
> And do it for them

Music ends. STEFAN exits to REBECCA's house. MIKE remains for a moment, but shakes his head and exits to the street.

ACT TWO   Scene Eight

Main Street in front of City Hall.

A throng of people, enter, marching silently, except for the sound of feet. They wear their Sunday best, with various assortment of hats. McDOUGALL and O'REILLY enter.

McDOUGALL   I feel like I'm on the wrong side of this crowd.

O'REILLY   Quiet, sir. It's a silent march. Hate to see them haul you in.

> *They join the march. MIKE enters, duffle bag in hand, and stands, listening to the growing sound of feet, thousands of them, marching. From off, a woman calls to her child.*

WOMAN   *(offstage)* Tekla! Tekla, get over here!

> *MIKE, startled, turns to look. People near the offstage voice shush her.*

STRIKER #1   Quiet – we have to be silent or they'll make arrests.

> *MIKE remains in the middle of it all, looking around him at determined faces on all sides.*

MIKE   *(to a MARCHER)* How many?

MARCHER   Ten thousand.

MIKE   Ten thousand and one.

> *Slowly, he begins to walk with them. Then marches. He becomes another face among them.*
>
> *In another part of the crowd, STEFAN and REBECCA enter, looking fearful but determined. They speak quietly among the silent faces.*

REBECCA   Thousands, Stefan. I want to see.

> *STEFAN lifts REBECCA. As she sees above the heads of the crowd, looking back over those still coming, her fear lifts.*

It's a field of people! Thousands and thousands! They're filling Main Street – past William Avenue… past Bannatyne… Portage Avenue… they're still coming…

> *She sees a face she recognizes.*

Oh, Stefan!

STEFAN   What is it?

REBECCA   *(to STEFAN)* Let me down!

STEFAN   Who?

> *As STEFAN sets REBECCA down, he looks up to see MIKE standing in front of him.*

Mike…

MIKE   Close your mouth. A bird will fly in.

REBECCA   You are with us?

MIKE   In Yiddish, sh-KEH-neh is the word for neighbour, yes?

REBECCA   Yes.

MIKE   Sh-KEH-neh help each other. Isn't that right, Miss Almazoff?

REBECCA   Yes.... Yes they do.

> *REBECCA hugs MIKE.*

STEFAN   Always.

> *STEFAN hugs MIKE. At that moment, the silence is broken with concerned murmurs over something happening offstage, and the bell and screeching wheels on steel of a streetcar.*

Look at this! The streetcars are on strike. Why does this one come?

CROWD   Scab, scab, scab! Provocation!

> *The crowd turns angry very quickly.*

STRIKER #1   Don't let it through!

STEFAN   It's deliberate provocation! They want a fight!

MIKE   Well, we don't have to give them one.

> *The crowd surges in the direction of the unseen streetcar. They yell encouragement to offstage STRIKERS.*

STRIKER #2   No scab labour!

STRIKER #3   Get the driver!

CROWD   Get the driver!

STEFAN   Tip the streetcar!

STRIKERS   Tip it over!

REBECCA   Stefan, stop it!

> *STEFAN tries to join the mob rushing the streetcar.*

STEFAN   Tip it!

REBECCA   Stefan! Come back!

MIKE   *(overlapping)* Stefan! Leave it alone!

> *SOLDIERS enter, CARMICHAEL at the lead, gun drawn and menacing. He fires his gun in the air several times getting everyone's attention.*

CARMICHAEL   The mayor has read the Riot Act. Disperse or suffer the consequences!

STRIKER #1   We're not leaving!

CROWD   No! We won't leave!

> *During the yelling, STEFAN has made his way back to MIKE and REBECCA.*

CARMICHAEL   Disperse this crowd immediately!

> *SOLDIERS directly in front of the crowd use their rifles to push the marchers back. One soldier hurts a marcher.*

STEFAN   You son of a bitch!

> *STEFAN picks up a brick.*

CARMICHAEL   Put down the brick Bolshevik!

REBECCA   Stefan, get away!

> *A second soldier swings his rifle around, pointing at STEFAN.*

CARMICHAEL   Put it down!

MIKE   Stefan!

> *REBECCA pulls STEFAN back. The second soldier cocks his rifle. REBECCA is now directly in his line of fire. MIKE steps in front of REBECCA.*

(to soldier) There are women and children here!

> *At the same moment, the second soldier begins shooting. The crowd screams and runs for cover.*

> *Music begins. [Play CD Track #19 – "Saturday in June."]*

> *MIKE is hit. He feels his chest, but finds himself still standing, watching as the crowd moves in confusion, and STEFAN and REBECCA catch his falling "body."*

> (singing) It wasn't supposed to end this way
> It wasn't supposed to be today
> On this Saturday in June
> I wasn't supposed to lose all face

It wasn't supposed to be this place
On this Saturday in June

I would have hoped for some-ting more
I could have fixed what I'd broke before
I could have done jus' what people do
On a Saturday in June

SPECIALS enter. They attack the marchers with clubs. STEFAN and REBECCA assist the unseen body in the place MIKE would have fallen.

But not on this
Saturday in June
How could I know
I'd have to go on this
Saturday in June?
Not a cloud in the sky
Barely a fight worth the time
On this Saturday
This Saturday in June

They weren't supposed to put us down
We were supposed to hold our ground
On this Saturday in June
There wasn't supposed to be blood spilled
There wasn't supposed to be any killed
On this Saturday in June
So many times I had run away
A better man needs to choose to stay
But what is the sense when lives are ruined
On a Saturday in June

O'REILLY and McDOUGALL join the battle as trained soldiers. They counter some SPECIALS but they too are overwhelmed and beaten down. EMMA, the Ashdown's maid, is among those in the crowd being beaten.

(angrily) Here on this
Saturday in June
How could I know
I'd have to go on this
Saturday in June?
Not a cloud in the sky
Barely a fight worth the time
On this Saturday
This Saturday in June

MIKE exits.

ALL But not on this
Saturday in June
How could we know
Where this would go on this
Saturday in June?
Not a cloud in the sky
Barely a fight worth the time
On this Saturday
This Saturday in June

The lights grow dim and the last to be seen are the SPECIALS, now firmly in control of the street.
Music ends.

ACT TWO   Epilogue

Brookside Cemetery, a few days later.

REBECCA and STEFAN stand before a grave. STEFAN pours a vial of dirt into the grave – a Ukrainian tradition of pouring dirt from the deceased's homeland. He makes the sign of the cross in the Ukrainian fashion, three times, three fingers together, crossing right to left.
A pause.

REBECCA We make speeches, we march, we stand up to them. For everything we believe in. And still soldiers come. Does it change? Does any of it change?

STEFAN It does, Rebecca Almazoff. It changes. We have to believe it. Or nothing makes sense.

REBECCA Nothing changes.

Pause. Then REBECCA begins the Kaddish, the prayer for the dead.

Yit-gah-DAHL ve-YIT-kah-dash she-MEH rah-BAH—

STEFAN surprises her by stopping her with a hand on her shoulder. He tries to repeat the Yiddish phrases.

STEFAN Yit-gah-DAHL ve-YIT-kah-dash… *(pause)* Please.

A beat as she absorbs what he is asking. And she begins teaching him.

REBECCA Yit-gah-DAHL ve-YIT-kah-dash she-MEH ra-BAH…

STEFAN   Yit-gah-DAHL ve-YIT-kah-dash SHE-meh ra-BAH…

REBECCA   Be'al-MAH di be-RAH…

STEFAN   Be'al-MAH di be-RAH…

> *His pronunciation is terrible, but together they speak the first lines of the Kaddish together.*

REBECCA   CHIR-u-teh VE-yam-lich MAL-chu-teh…

STEFAN   CHIR-u-teh VE-yam-lich MAL-chu-teh…

REBECCA   be-cha-YE-chon uv-yo-ME-chon…

STEFAN   be-cha-YE-chon uv-yo-ME-chon…

REBECCA   u-ve-cha-YEY de-CHOL bet YIS-ra-el

STEFAN   u-ve-cha-YEY de-CHOL bet YIS-ra-el

REBECCA   ba-ah-ga-LAH u-VEES-man ka-REEV veem-RU ah-MAIN

STEFAN   ba-ah-ga-LAH u-VEES-man ka-REEV veem-RU ah-MAIN

> *She squeezes his hand in thanks. He moves to leave, but she doesn't.*

REBECCA   I get a chance too, yes?

> *Pause. STEFAN begins the Our Father.*

STEFAN   OH-cheh nash, TE-shcho yeh seh…

REBECCA   OH-cheh nash, TE-shcho yeh seh…

STEFAN   NAH neh-boh-SACH…

REBECCA   NAH neh-boh-SACH…

> *They continue to stumble through the prayer together, their voices fading as the scene shifts.*

STEFAN   Neh-CHIY shva-TET-shva…

REBECCA   Neh-CHIY shva-TET-shva…

> *The Board of Trade Building, Central Winnipeg, a few days later.*
>
> *Music begins. [Play CD Track #20 – "Epilogue."]*
>
> *SUSAN addresses an unseen audience. It is a passionate speech, suggesting a new decision, the beginning of an entirely new phase in SUSAN's life.*

SUSAN   Let us be frank. Let us call a spade a spade. And let us not gloat in what some mistake for victory. For we preside over a city, indeed a nation, divided. There is a gulf in the land, a chasm between those of means, and those of none. Change beckons angrily across that chasm, and we must heed its call or risk the ridicule, and the terror, of the future, where scorn will freely flow in our absence.

Portage Avenue, two months later.

WALLACE darts across the stage, elated.

WALLACE   He's free. Almazoff is free!

A crowd gathers. MOISHE ALMAZOFF enters on the shoulders of his supporters, including McDOUGALL and O'REILLY. MOISHE addresses his supporters.

MOISHE   *(to the crowd)* This is my home! This is where I choose to live my life! And here are those who are dearest to me. Let us never apologize for who we are and where we come from, and when others attempt to deny us, remember this day and every day of those who came before you.

> *(singing)* An immigrant is all they see
> An alien, the enemy
> Yes immigrants we all may be but
> Seize the hour and
> Show them our
> Unity

REBECCA and STEFAN are last to run in – they hug MOISHE in reunion.

ALL
> An immigrant is all they see
> An alien, the enemy
> An immigrant yes I may be
> But damn them all
> I'll die with all
> My dignity
> Damn them all
> I'll die with all
> My dignity

Music Continues. [Allow Track #20 to continue playing through to Track #21 – "Strike! Reprise."]

> Strike while the iron's hot to
> Get what we haven't got and
> Take back the things they took and
> Make right the wrongs and look right
> Into their eyes until they blink realizin' that we

Won't give up the fight no so
Muster up your might and strike!

Music ends. Final curtain.

Rick Chafe's plays include his new adaptation of *Shakespeare's Dog* (adapted from Leon Rooke's Governor General's Literary Award-winning novel), *The Odyssey, The Last Man and Woman on Earth,* and *Zac and Speth.* Rick also works as a dramaturge, television story consultant and writer, produces documentary video, and has taught playwriting to every age of student from grade one to university. He lives in Winnipeg with his wife and their nine-year-old daughter.

Dubbed "Canada's Andrew Lloyd Webber," **Danny Schur** is Winnipeg's most successful composer/producer of original musicals. Having made his name as a Juno Award-winning composer/producer (Chantal Kreviazuk, Doc Walker) Danny turned his sights on his true passion: original musical theatre. His musical *The Bridge* was Winnipeg's first full-scale original musical and *Strike!* earned Danny & co-writer, Rick Chafe, the 2006 Kobzar™ Literary Award and the 2007 Grant MacEwan College Kostash Award. The pair have written the screenplay adaptation of *Strike!* and a feature film is in pre-production.

To remove CD, cut envelope along top edge.
Return CD to envelope for storage.

The book may not be returned if the CD has been
removed, or an attempt has been made to remove it.